Teaching Dilemmas and Solutions in
CONTENT-AREA
LITERACY
GRADES 6–12

Teaching Dilemmas and Solutions in
CONTENT-AREA LITERACY
GRADES 6–12

edited by

PETER SMAGORINSKY

CORWIN
A SAGE Company

CORWIN
A SAGE Company

FOR INFORMATION:

Corwin
A SAGE Company
2455 Teller Road
Thousand Oaks, California 91320
(800) 233-9936
www.corwin.com

SAGE Publications Ltd.
1 Oliver's Yard
55 City Road
London EC1Y 1SP
United Kingdom

SAGE Publications India Pvt. Ltd.
B 1/I 1 Mohan Cooperative Industrial Area
Mathura Road, New Delhi 110 044
India

SAGE Publications Asia-Pacific Pte. Ltd.
3 Church Street
#10-04 Samsung Hub
Singapore 049483

Acquisitions Editor: Carol Collins
Development Editor: Renee Nicholls
Editorial Development Manager: Julie Nemer
Editorial Assistant: Francesca Dutra Africano
Production Editor: Veronica Stapleton Hooper
Copy Editor: Lana Todorovic-Arndt
Typesetter: C&M Digitals (P) Ltd.
Proofreader: Scott Oney
Indexer: Molly Hall
Cover Designer: Gail Buschman
Marketing Manager: Maura Sullivan

Library of Congress Cataloging-in-Publication Data

Smagorinsky, Peter.

Teaching dilemmas and solutions in content-area literacy, grades 6-12 / Peter Smagorinsky, University of Georgia.

pages cm
Includes bibliographical references and index.

ISBN 978-1-4522-2993-5 (pbk. : alk. paper)

1. English language—Writing—Study and teaching (Secondary) 2. Literacy—Study and teaching (Secondary) I. Title.

LB1631.S525 2014
428.0071′2—dc23   2014009492

This book is printed on acid-free paper.

14 15 16 17 18 10 9 8 7 6 5 4 3 2 1

Contents

Introduction

Peter Smagorinsky

A few years back, I interviewed teachers as part of a study of writing across the high school curriculum. When asked about the difference between writing in science and writing in English classes, a chemistry teacher said that English and science teachers have very different expectations for writers. To illustrate, he described an assignment he'd given his students in which they were responsible for researching and reporting on the contributions of a notable scientist. The students, he said, would try and make their writing creative and humorous, as if they were writing for an English teacher. In contrast, he said, science writing is straightforward and based on factual evidence, which must be marshalled into an analysis and scientific interpretation. The point in science writing, he continued, isn't to express personal opinions. Although aspects of writing like grammar carry over from English to science writing, the styles are different. In particular, scientists rely on figures and diagrams, often in place of prose explanations that might confuse the issues rather than clarify them. Figures, in contrast, are direct and unencumbered by the complexities of language, which he believed muddled the concepts being taught. For a literate scientist, knowing and understanding how to produce and read a clear diagram is far more important than being fluent with the expressive writing required by English teachers.

This teacher identified a central problem in school learning: What a student learns in one class may not be appropriate for what a teacher expects in another. Science, he argued, depends on precision and the understanding of scientific concepts that are often most clearly and effectively explained by diagrams of how elements and objects move and interact. Written explanations of the sort expected by English teachers may not be appropriate; in fact, they may actually be confusing compared with other ways of representing information for the purposes of scientific understanding. Indeed, the more like the writing encouraged by English teachers the explanation may be—with creativity, opinions, feelings, unique vocabulary, metaphorical expression, and other rhetorical moves valued in the humanities—the less effective it may be in teaching and expressing scientific concepts.

Contrary, then, to a belief among many educators that "writing is writing," not only are expectations for what writers do different from class to class; writing may only be part of what counts as a literate expression in some fields of study. In order to serve students well across the curriculum, it is thus important for teachers and administrators to understand that an approach to literacy that works very well in one disciplinary application may need significant adaptation for the next. This book is designed to use literacy narratives from different academic disciplines to illustrate what teachers benefit from knowing about literacy expectations within their own fields and to know what students must be aware of when they head down the hallway for a class that relies on different assumptions about clear and appropriate expression.

ABOUT THIS BOOK

Whether you are a teacher, an administrator, a curriculum specialist, a literacy coach, or just a reader with a keen interest in the topic at hand, this book is designed to illuminate for you what it means to know and be literate in different disciplines across the secondary school curriculum. *Merriam Webster*'s dictionary defines *discipline* as "a rule or system of rules governing conduct or activity" ("Discipline," 2003). It is derived from the Latin words *disciplina* and *discipulus,* which refer to teaching, learning, and pupil. Together, these roots and meanings suggest that each discipline has evolved a system of rules that frame the ways in which people think and communicate with one another. As the example at the beginning of this introduction shows, the rules that are developed among scientists for precise and straightforward communication of concepts are different from those that govern the more figurative and open-ended domain of English. Furthermore, each field has developed values and ways of using symbol systems that distinguish them from other disciplines as well. In this book, the contributors provide a disciplinary approach to being literate across the most commonly occurring subjects in the secondary school curriculum in which the composition and reading of texts is a central activity in developing subject-area competence.

How This Book Is Organized

The book focuses on the disciplines of English, History, Science, Mathematics, Visual Space, and Music and Drama, with a chapter devoted to each. The goal is not to cover every possible area of literate performance within a school, but to focus on those most likely to be taught with an academic emphasis. This emphasis includes specific expectations for how to think by engaging with texts, whether they are verbal or produced through a visual, aural, or spatial medium.

In addition to being organized by subject area, each of the chapters in this book has been written to follow the same internal structure, providing you with

- a review of literacy issues relevant to the focal discipline,
- vignettes that capture a series of fundamental disciplinary dilemmas for which the teachers attempt a solution, and
- essential questions that follow from the dilemmas presented in the vignettes.

The vignettes are designed to foster discussion about the degree to which the solution would be effective within your particular school setting. If you find that the solution would not work for you and your students, then we encourage you to identify options that might be more appropriate. In this way, the book is designed to promote collaboration with your colleagues about what disciplinary literacy involves and about which literacy practices are shared across disciplines. The goal of these discussions, which will be explained in more depth in the next section, is to help you and your colleagues move toward better understandings of literacy in its full academic breadth and of how to teach appropriate disciplinary literacy skills effectively.

How to Use This Book

The authors of the chapters that follow believe that one of the best ways for schools to align their instructional programs with the Common Core or other mandates, and to achieve other social and academic goals, is to foster *thoughtful* and *substantive conversations* among a school's faculty. In particular, these discussions should focus on

- the nature of literacy within each discipline,
- the most effective ways to promote literacy within each discipline,
- thoughtful ways to measure student progress over time, and
- steps to ensure that all teachers across the disciplines see themselves as teachers of literacy who can help all students become more engaged and literate citizens.

Teaching Dilemmas and Solutions in Content-Area Literacy is written to make this vision a reality in diverse schools and to honor their unique mix of students, teachers, and circumstances.

Although this book is available for individual reading and consideration, it will have the greatest impact if it is used as a medium for discussion. We suggest that you form study groups of professional learning communities dedicated to reflecting on local practices of teaching and learning. You can then use each chapter of this text to augment and inform the important work of collecting and considering the evidence of student learning that drives your decisions about curriculum and instruction.

WHAT DOES IT MEAN TO BE LITERATE?

There was a time, and not so long ago, when adults were considered literate if they could sign a document with an "X" (Reay, 1991). As education has succeeded in providing compulsory and comprehensive education to U.S. citizens, expectations have grown for what a literate person can do. The Common Core State Standards, for instance, include CCSS. ELA-Literacy.W.K.1, which requires kindergarten students to "use a combination of drawing, dictating, and writing to compose opinion pieces in which they tell a reader the topic or the name of the book they are writing about and state an opinion or preference about the topic or book (e.g., *My favorite book is* . . .)" (Copyright © 2010 National Governors Association Center for Best Practices and Council of Chief State School Officers).

The Common Core State Standards, around which many curricula are now organized, is centered on language as the primary medium of expression and literacy. This emphasis is at odds with conceptions of literacy that now include the reading and composing of texts of all sorts, including the diagrams that are valued in the various scientific fields and that are essential in arts and those disciplines involving graphic texts. In my own research, for instance, I've studied high school classes such as architectural design (Smagorinsky, Cook, & Reed, 2005) and nonverbal composing in English such as pictorial representations of literary action (Smagorinsky & Coppock, 1994). The first of these comprises an act of disciplinary literacy; the second represented an arts-oriented teacher's hybrid view of what English might include if it expanded its historical emphases beyond the printed word.

In each case, being literate included composing through texts that involved more than words. The historical definition of literacy—originating in the Latin word *litteratus,* meaning marked with letters—has undergone considerable rethinking in light of expanded understandings of what it means to compose a text. I have found that the definition of literacy offered by Scribner and Cole (1981) has held up quite well over time. They defined literacy as

> a set of socially organized practices which make use of a symbol system and a technology for producing and disseminating it. Literacy is not simply knowing how to read and write a particular script but applying this knowledge for specific purposes in specific contexts of use. The nature of these practices, including, of course, their technological aspects, will determine the kinds of skills ("consequences") associated with literacy. (p. 236)

This definition suggests that literacy is a multifaceted concept that cannot be taught solely within one discipline (typically English) and then exported wholly for use in others. Rather, contexts of usage bring their own demands to how literacy is performed. In school, these contexts include different academic disciplines and their special traditions and expectations. They might also include very local interpretations of a discipline, such as when the teacher encouraged artistic interpretations of stories through art. Outside the classroom, contexts produce considerable variation in literacy practices, ranging from the arcane terminology of football teams—which is often so local that only team members know its cryptic meanings so as to mask intentions to opponents—to the special language employed by tax lawyers. Being literate in one area is often of little use to grasping concepts in others. This conundrum is at work in schools and is at the heart of the issues raised in this book.

CONTENT-AREA LITERACY

This book is aligned with a recent report by the National Center for Literacy Education (NCLE, 2013) and its recommendations for teachers. The rest of this section highlights the key findings of this report and explains how the book is designed to help schools meet their imperative for advancing the literacy fluency of the nation's students.

Implications for Practice

The NCLE report provides five major findings, which I condense here into four implications for practice.

Literacy is not just the English teacher's job anymore. There is often a belief that students learn to read and write in English classes, and then they apply those skills across the curriculum. This idea has been under fire for some time because, as the chemistry teacher's earlier remarks suggest, each discipline has its own values and means of expression. Science teachers cannot rely on English teachers to teach the ways of using language and other symbols that scientists rely on to convey ideas clearly and efficiently, because English teachers are trained in the humanities, with their literary orientation and interpretive flair. While English teachers might be able to provide a basic understanding of how sentences and paragraphs are constructed, they are less able to teach their students how to think and represent knowledge in math or history, especially when the value systems that govern expression in those other disciplines are different.

Rather, teachers in each discipline need to emphasize what makes their work unique and how their ways of reading and writing require special knowledge. The chapter in this book on mathematics, for instance, stresses the unique definition of "plane" that mathematicians use and the various symbols through which the characteristics of planes are expressed and calculated. Literacy thus extends beyond syntax and grammar and includes specialized vocabularies, the appropriate use of graphics such as maps and diagrams, and other expectations for engagement with disciplinary texts and the understandings they convey.

Working together is working smarter, yet barriers exist. Although the idea of "working smarter" is perhaps overused and, in such features as the Dilbert comic strip, subject to satire, the authors of the NCLE report emphasize the importance of collaboration among faculty members in the development of curriculum and instruction. Unfortunately, in many cases schools are not structured to foster collaboration, because teachers are isolated from one another with all-day demands for teaching, planning, grading, patrolling hallways and parking lots, monitoring cafeterias and study halls, and serving in other duties. As a result, opportunities for collaborative planning in these schools are rare and precious occasions. Schools hoping to promote more opportunities for collaboration have attempted to create space by scheduling common planning periods, grade-level lunch times, and other within-day spaces, although these inevitably get compromised and usurped by other priorities and demands. Creating such spaces would seem to be incumbent on administrators who believe in the value of faculty conversations about their work.

Many of the building blocks for remodeling literacy learning are in place. Even with the institutional barriers that work against collaborative planning, some features are in place that may facilitate teamwork in advancing the school's literacy mission. These include

- structures such as grade-level, subject-area, and data-driven assessment teams that could provide means for discussions of literacy education;

- online tools that may enable collaboration when other factors miti-
  gate against face-to-face meetings;
- a value on collaboration that is often shared, if not always available,
  among teachers; and
- access to literacy coaches and other sorts of curriculum supervisors,
  whose job is designed to promote discussions across disciplinary
  and other boundaries.

These structures, and perhaps others, can be adapted to promote the
sort of discussions that will benefit the advancement of any curriculum
and instruction development. Moreover, they can be employed, along with
professional learning opportunities, to address the issues raised in this
book.

Effective collaboration needs systemic support. The NCLE report
encourages schools to establish collaboration as the norm for developing
more effective teaching practices, with administrators and others in formal
and informal leadership positions helping to facilitate cooperative instructional efforts by providing time, training, and appropriate tools.

Policy Recommendations

In the NCLE report, policymakers are defined as those who, at the
school, system, state, and national levels, play a central role in remodeling literacy education. Policymakers at all levels, they argue, should do
the following:

- Support teachers in their understanding of their own discipline's
  specific literacy demands.
- Build opportunities for collaboration into the school day by including systemic structures (e.g., shared planning periods or lunch
  times) that enable productive discussions to occur.
- Support ongoing, job-embedded, and collaborative professional
  learning by providing whatever funds, time, and space are needed
  to achieve it.
- Encourage accountability by using these professional discussions to
  identify what is involved in successful literacy teaching and learning and how to document student growth in valid ways.

I have been in and around a variety of schools in a number of states
over the last three-and-a-half decades, including substitute teaching in
Trenton, New Jersey, and Chicago public schools; teaching in three suburban high schools outside Chicago; and teaching, supervising, and studying teachers in Illinois, Oklahoma, and Georgia. I have seen the sort of

savage inequalities that Jonathan Kozol (1992) has described between affluent and impoverished districts and the indomitable spirit that enables teachers to endure the most desperate of teaching circumstances in order to make kids' lives better. I know that the literacy recommendations of the NCLE and the idealistic expectations of the Common Core State Standards can seem out of reach for schools in which time for collaboration and the possibilities for widespread literacy development are distant hopes. The majority of schools in Georgia, for instance, annually "furlough" teachers for ten to thirty school days because they can't afford to run a full school year, much less do so with the luxuries that enable the achievement of ideal outcomes. I do not suggest that this book will enable communities to transcend their circumstances or wave a magic wand over their populace to produce new revenue streams or full employment for their students' families.

At the same time, the book is designed to be hopeful in its intentions and the practices it promotes. It is also my personal hope that the conversations stimulated by these chapters will serve to make school a more satisfying and rewarding experience, both for the teachers and administrators who engage in them, and for the students who reap the benefits of the new ideas that they generate.

Note to the reader: The scenarios that appear throughout this book have been fictionalized; they are not intended to represent specific schools or classroom situations. They are composites of classroom scenarios that the contributors have experienced throughout their years of teaching or encountered in their research.

REFERENCES

Discipline. (2003). In *Merriam-Webster's collegiate dictionary* (11th ed., electronic version). Springfield, MA: Merriam-Webster.

Kozol, J. (1992). *Savage inequalities: Children in America's schools.* New York, NY: Harper Perennial.

National Center for Literacy Education. (2013). *Remodeling literacy learning: Making room for what works.* Urbana, IL: National Center for Literacy Education & National Council of Teachers of English. Retrieved from www.literacyin learningexchange.org/sites/default/files/ncle_report_final_format_0.pdf

National Governors Association (NGA) Center for Best Practices, & the Council of Chief State School Officers (CCSSO). (2010). *Common core state standards initiative.* Washington, DC: Author. Retrieved from http://www.corestandards .org/assets/CCSSI_ELA%20Standards.pdf

Reay, B. (1991). The context and meaning of popular literacy: Some evidence from nineteenth-century rural England. *Past and Present, 131*(1), 89–129.

Scribner, S., & Cole, M. (1981). *The psychology of literacy.* Cambridge, MA: Harvard University Press.

Smagorinsky, P., Cook, L., & Reed, P. (2005). The construction of meaning and identity in the composition and reading of an architectural text. *Reading Research Quarterly, 40,* 70–88. Retrieved from www.petersmagorinsky.net/About/PDF/RRQ/RRQ2005.pdf

Smagorinsky, P., & Coppock, J. (1994). Cultural tools and the classroom context: An exploration of an alternative response to literature. *Written Communication, 11,* 283–310. Retrieved from www.petersmagorinsky.net/About/PDF/WC/WC1994.pdf

Literacy in the English/Language Arts Classroom

Peter Smagorinsky and Joseph M. Flanagan

Not so long ago, literacy in English classes was fairly straightforward. The discipline was built on a foundation of three strands: reading (mostly of literature), writing, and language/grammar. Most knowledge in these areas concerned understanding proper form. Literature was understood as the sum of its elements, and knowing these elements served as the basis for literary instruction. Teachers thus focused on plot, characterization, conflict, figures of speech, foreshadowing, point of view, symbolism, theme, tone, and many curriculum document pages' worth of other terms and techniques that would lead students to acceptable interpretations of canonical literature. The study of grammar concerned the labeling of various parts of sentences, which presumably led to proper usage. Writing consisted of a set of genres—description, narration, exposition, persuasion, definition—that students produced by studying the features of model compositions.

CHANGING CONCEPTIONS OF LITERACY

Although much instruction in English classes retains these values and emphases, the discipline has been complicated by a number of developments both within the field and without. The advent of the personal computer, for instance, produced great changes in how people communicate. Early personal computers served primarily as word processors. As computer memory began to increase exponentially with each new generation of machines, however, digital capabilities provided new ways of representing ideas through graphics, animation, video, sound, and other options. The development of the Internet provided new platforms for using these technologies, which soon became available on smaller devices, including phones, tablets, and other media.

Now that many students—at least those affluent enough to afford these technologies—have the ability to compose digital texts, definitions of what makes a person literate in society have changed. The field of "New Literacies Studies" has produced such terms as *multimodality* and *multiliteracies* and invigorated interest in *semiotics,* the study of sign systems, including both language and other ways of representing and communicating ideas. The primary medium of communication in these modes is the Internet, and because it provides students with access to material that is both clearly and not-so-clearly inappropriate for school, new ways to cheat and plagiarize, and other possibilities, teachers now struggle to determine the degree to which such opportunities should be available for schoolwork.

THE GROWING DEBATE REGARDING WHAT STUDENTS SHOULD BE READING

Another recent debate involves the literary canon, which has also come under reconsideration. Lists of frequently taught texts still include the usual suspects: Shakespeare, Twain, Hawthorne, and other standard-bearers of the literature curriculum. But teachers have also advocated for the inclusion of not-yet-canonical texts from the Young Adult Literature (YAL) repertoire so that in addition to reading literature written long ago in archaic language about enduring themes, students read books of more immediate relevance and interest. Graphic novels as well have become popular and provocative, if not always appropriate for school. YAL novels tend to focus on the issues that affect current youth: relationships, temptations, sexuality, bullying, technology, substance abuse, divorce, conflicts, and other experiences of today's world. This content, which frequently reflects students' real, complicated, and precarious lives, has made such books controversial in school settings. They represent quite a departure from the adult world described in literature from past eras that teachers, administrators, and parents are likely to have encountered in their own school experiences and so are a more familiar and comfortable fit for their expectations, even in the bawdy world of Shakespeare.

Deciding how to address the chasm between the historical themes of canonical literature and the developmentally appropriate themes of YAL continues to vex English faculty and contribute to disagreements about how the subject should be taught.

THE TRANSFORMATION OF INSTRUCTIONAL STRATEGIES FOR ENGLISH LANGUAGE ARTS

The *how* of literature instruction has also changed. The historic image of the English teacher is the "sage on the stage": the teacher standing before rows of students explaining the meaning of literature. However, the emphasis on learning processes that got traction in the 1960s and became central to educational theory in subsequent decades raised questions about the value of lecture-oriented instruction focused on technical knowledge of form. This teaching method served as the core approach of "New Criticism," the dominant critical paradigm for many decades (Applebee, 1993). Various pedagogies under the name of "Reader Response" teaching challenged the assumption that technical knowledge of literary form should provide the basis of literature instruction. Although many of these approaches involved somewhat of an "anything goes" classroom, other teaching methods in the *constructivist* mode relied on students to make meaning of texts through personal connections in ways that were clearly linked to the textual content and form (Beach, 1993). This alternative contributed to a growing rift between those who align themselves according to a series of related binaries: product or process, received knowledge or constructed knowledge, cultural heritage or personal growth, and other divides over what to emphasize in teaching literature. Although these oppositions obscure the fact that most teachers reside in the middle rather than at the extremes, for most educators, the tensions have remained over how to conduct classroom business.

Language instruction too became contested ground. For much of the discipline's history, language instruction involved understanding sentence structure (Weaver, 1996). This knowledge included knowing the eight parts of speech and understanding their relationships within the confines of the sentence. Textbooks prescribed proper grammatical constructions and rules of use, and instruction centered on making sure students knew these constructions and could identify them in sentences, typically sentences written by someone else and presented in a grammar and composition textbook.

Linguists, however, began to question the validity of this approach to language instruction. Many argued that different cultural groups had internally consistent dialects or speech genres that, even though they violated textbook rules, were suitable for communication within social groups—even more suitable than the "standard" language structure specified in the textbooks. This perspective was realized most prominently in debates about what to do with the colloquial speech of African American students, which has variously been labeled African American Vernacular English, African American English, Black English, Ebonics, and other names (Alim & Baugh, 2006; Kinloch, 2010). The National Council of Teachers of English, in 1977, adopted a position about "Students' Right to Their Own Language." This position endorsed the potential of linguistic diversity and recognized the reality of "communicative competence": the fact that what matters in communication is adherence to local, rather than universal, rules. The recent waves of immigrants who have formed hybrid dialects such as "Spanglish" further challenge the belief that there is a single form of English that suits all people in all situations.

Although the perspective of linguistic diversity has been widely accepted, grammar instruction in English classes remains focused on proper sentence form. In fact, this emphasis has persisted in spite of the consensus from research findings for well over a century that direct instruction in grammatical concepts, at least when taught in isolation from language use, has little or no effect on students' speech or writing (Hillocks, 1986; Weaver, 1996). The dispute remains associated with the broader product-versus-process debate. Historically, students have been evaluated on their ability to demonstrate linguistic understanding evaluating sentences written by others. This approach allows scorers to evaluate the student work numerically but is not tied to students' own writing. Although alternatives are available that rely on students' generative capabilities (e.g., through such means as sentence-combining exercises, in which students take given clauses and phrases and rewrite them to produce whole new sentences), the results can be difficult to evaluate on a standardized test. This dilemma is present in nearly every aspect of the English curriculum: the amenability of student work to be tested and reduced to a numeric score versus the value of instruction to improve students' situation-specific linguistic performances.

Writing instruction has paralleled both literary and grammatical teaching with respect to the product-versus-process debate. "Traditional" writing instruction is oriented to correct essay form, often in five paragraphs: an introductory thesis, three body paragraphs, and a conclusion (see Johnson, Smagorinsky, Thompson, & Fry, 2003). Teachers present students with models with the features labeled and then instruct the class to reproduce the form in their own writing. Yet the "process revolution" of recent decades has questioned the degree to which students can learn processes and strategies by studying completed products, and it has produced a variety of process-oriented alternatives (Smagorinsky, Johannessen, Kahn, & McCann, 2010). The most liberating of these approaches (and the one that has the most potential to frustrate students of weak entry-level writing preparation) relies on students' self-directed composing. In this approach, teachers may unleash students in "workshop" settings where the learners choose what to write and how to write about it, with the teacher serving primarily to help students set and meet their writing goals and to provide feedback when requested. Other process-oriented approaches require more planning by the teacher to set up particular tasks to help students learn defined strategies for specific types of writing. This view follows the assumption that writing a narrative involves different knowledge and procedures than does writing an argument, and so forth. This perspective gets undermined when a state writing test evaluates all writing according to a single five-paragraph-theme rubric, as is the case in several states (Hillocks, 2002).

Writing has grown yet more complex by the availability of a greater variety of genres and the possibilities of incorporating more than one genre into a single piece of writing. As noted, the availability of technology to produce texts further complicates older conceptions of writing, especially when the question of relevance is considered. Students rarely write five-paragraph themes anywhere but in an English class, and it is not clear what their adult worlds will require of them. Creating multimedia websites might indeed be of greater value to twenty-first-century students than writing five-paragraph themes. If students are to be viewed as literate in the world that awaits them tomorrow, then teachers are challenged today to consider what literacies will be involved in that future setting (Hicks, 2013).

FORGING A PATH FOR LITERACY INSTRUCTION

Literacy education in English classes thus stands at a challenging juncture. As a teacher, there is much that you need to consider, including the degree to which

- old-world literacies provide the framework for new-world competencies,
- historic modes of communication remain robust in the current century, and
- new technologies represent fads or enduring trends.

The vignettes that follow capture some of the dilemmas facing teachers of English/Language Arts today. Specifically, they are designed to prompt you to consider factors such as

- how you will decide what counts as literate performance in school,
- how that performance will serve students in their lives,
- how the constraints of classroom settings influence the decisions you make, and
- how your teaching fits in politically with your community and school social worlds.

Following each vignette, we provide some rationale for the teachers' decisions, along with a set of questions for your reflection. Your response to these questions, ideally discussed with colleagues, should help you to frame your own theory of what counts as appropriate literacy instruction and performance in the discipline of the English/Language Arts.

SCENARIOS

SCENARIO 1: Language Proficiency as Literacy

The setting: A middle-track ninth-grade English class at Floodrock High School, a suburban school that graduates 80 percent of its students. Roughly half of the graduating students go on to attend a two- or four-year college; half of them ultimately earn college degrees. Of the remaining students, half enter the workforce directly and half join the military or attend some kind of trade school.

The characters: Sonja Lee's ninth graders represent the overall demographics of the school. Forty percent of the students are European American, 25 percent are African American, 20 percent are Latino/a, 10 percent are Asian American, and 5 percent identify as mixed race. Forty-five percent of the students receive free or reduced-cost breakfast and lunch at the school, and 10 percent are enrolled in an ESL/bilingual education program.

Sonja recently wrote her master's thesis on language diversity and dialects, taking the position that students' home languages should be honored as their primary speech genres. Her university professors passed her thesis with distinction.

Sonja's colleagues in other academic departments frequently complain that many of the students don't speak proper English. These colleagues are quite vocal in blaming the English teachers, claiming that they must not be doing their jobs.

Sonja often eats lunch with a colleague, Paula Raszinski, who regards herself as the school's resident grammarian. Paula teaches all tenth-grade classes, and when students do not know grammar entering her class, she blames the ninth-grade teachers at department meetings. Believing that "we have to hold these students accountable for their own learning," Paula docks students one full letter grade in any assignment for each error in grammar, punctuation, or usage.

The context: Like most of the teachers she knows, Sonja engages in a great deal of professional reading. Through these efforts, she has learned that more than a century's worth of research on teaching grammar overwhelmingly concludes that teaching grammar in isolation from usage does not improve students' writing proficiency as measured on tests. Similarly, she has read that forcing students to speak the standard variety of English does not result in raised test scores. In the past, Sonja always believed that the study of grammar had a direct impact on student writing, but now she has changed her classroom instruction accordingly.

While Sonja has altered her teaching practices to align with the research, many of her colleagues have rejected the professional findings, arguing that university professors' research is out of touch with classroom realities. Most continue to teach grammar as a subject unto itself and then grade their students' writing based on their fidelity to what has been emphasized in the grammar exercises.

Sonja works tirelessly to meet the needs of her students but finds herself under pressure from the school district to increase test scores. Recent changes in tenure laws have left Sonja, and other teachers, fearful that heads will roll soon if scores don't rise. In a recent article in the local paper, the president of the board of education, a businesswoman in town, stressed the notion of teacher accountability and pushed for annual yearly progress, arguing, "The stock market goes up every year, why shouldn't students' test scores?" She also asserted that school officials would be paying closer attention to test scores, graduation rates, and other indicators of productivity as a means of judging teacher performance. Teachers, she stated, are service providers and must be held accountable for the quality of their educational product lest they be replaced by someone with a better understanding of the relation between input and output.

Sonja's colleagues often refer to the state curriculum guide to align their course-work with state standards. With the growing pressure from the district, Sonja often finds herself doing so as well. The state document includes many pages of references to grammatical knowledge that teachers at each grade level are responsible for teaching in order for students to pass end-of-course and graduation exams. In keeping with the traditional view of grammar instruction, Sonja's English department curriculum requires the use of a commercial grammar and composition textbook as part of the classroom instruction. Sonja finds that many of her students struggle with the lessons in the grammar and composition textbook. In their everyday speech, a lot of the ninth graders speak different dialects. Although each dialect follows its own rules consistently, few dialects follow the rules detailed in the textbook.

This inconsistency has also created turbulence in the community. An organization of African American parents has petitioned the school to have Ebonics recognized as their children's first language. They want standard English treated as the kids' second language, which would require a special course taught within the ESL/ bilingual curriculum, and funded by that budget line. An organization of Latino/a parents has further requested that each subject be taught in a "dual immersion" environment, in which all students study each subject in both English and Spanish.

These proposals have garnered the attention of several groups within the community, some more pleased with the diversity at Floodrock High School than others. An organization within the county that opposes illegal immigration is now pressuring the school board to verify each student's residence and citizenship status and to allow only "Standard English" to be spoken in the school building for classes and extracurricular activities. Recently, the Parent-Teacher Association produced a position paper arguing that all students need access to success in the economy and that correct use of English is a fundamental requirement of such access. A senior in AP English found six errors of grammar, punctuation, and usage in the document, gave the position paper a failing grade, and posted it on her social media webpage, after which the posting went viral in the district and community.

The dilemma: Sonja needs to decide how to teach her class so that her students "succeed" in the grammar strand of the English curriculum. She wants to achieve the following:

- satisfy the administration so that she keeps her job,
- satisfy parents so that they do not barrage her with complaints and petitions,
- respond to research and theory so that her teaching is aligned with the field's knowledge base,
- meet her students' authentic learning needs,
- act as a good citizen of her school and department, and
- provide her students with the skills they need to position themselves for success in whatever direction they take later in school and in life.

The "solution": Sonja decides to teach the language strand so that it serves students' communicative needs. She plans to focus on the rhetorical expectations for each communicative situation and to create reasonably authentic opportunities for students to express themselves in relation to each set of readers or listeners. She therefore sets up speaking opportunities that in turn lead to writing opportunities, and she links each language episode to both the literature and writing strands of the curriculum.

For example, the curriculum requires that the students read *To Kill a Mockingbird*. It also requires comparison and contrast essays for ninth grade. Sonja decides to teach students to compare and contrast different characters' perspectives on issues of racial equality, a theme that is central to the novel and also is tied to local issues of employment, housing, immigration status, and other aspects of life in the community. In conjunction with their reading of the novel, she begins with having students compare and contrast the perspectives on racial equality of different social groups within the school. Students use graphic organizers to identify groups with different perspectives, compare and contrast those perspectives according to a set of dimensions, and arrive at a value judgment about the perspectives being compared and contrasted. Finally, students draft documents addressed to an audience of their choice, using their writing to discuss and identify rhetorical expectations. Students write their papers in the following forms: as an opinion piece to be published in the city's newspaper, as a recommendation to the board of education on how to improve race relationships in the school, as an open letter to students on how to improve race relationships, as a letter to a friend from another city recommending whether or not the friend should transfer to their school, and as a blog entry posted on a youth issues website. Following the completion of the papers, students compare and contrast the rhetorical demands of each readership, how well the papers meet the needs of their designated readerships, and how the different readers provide different expectations for student writers.

During the class's reading of *To Kill a Mockingbird*, Sonja continually has the students compare and contrast different characters' and social groups' attitudes about racial equality. Following their reading, she has the class apply the strategies of comparing and contrasting, rhetorical analysis, and composing within readers' expectations. Groups of students discuss how to analyze and write about two different characters' or social groups' attitudes about race and use graphic organizers to set up their ideas. Then each student writes his or her own comparison and contrast paper analyzing the points of view of selected characters or social groups, directed toward a particular, well-defined readership. Following the students' composition of the papers, Sonja leads the class in a discussion of which conventions are appropriate to follow for each writing situation.

The rationale for the instruction: Sonja's teaching is based on the premise that although the curriculum has three distinct strands—literature, writing, and language—they should be taught in conjunction with one another. She therefore addresses grammar instruction as part of an integrated pedagogy in which the language strand is taught in the context of students' "audience awareness" of the rhetorical expectations of different sets of readers in their writing.

Sonja's attention to grammar does not come in isolated exercises or drills that focus on labeling parts of sentences. Rather, she views grammatical knowledge as a feature of rhetoric, and rhetoric as a feature of writing. She understands that she is sacrificing the labeling aspect of grammatical study, even though she uses some terms to help emphasize how her students can persuade their readers of their perspective (e.g., she instructs them to "use action verbs"). She believes, however, that once out of school, her students will continue to try to persuade people of their opinions, but they will not take any more standardized grammar tests. Under that assumption, she teaches grammar as a communication device, although she recognizes that some of her colleagues continue to believe that students only learn grammar when teachers focus on it as an independent area of study.

She links her teaching of these essays to the study of *To Kill a Mockingbird*. As noted, she encourages students to take a structured approach to the writing process by asking them to use graphic organizers to help them think about the problems they will write about. Students then discuss these organizers in small groups prior to beginning their essays. These collaborative groups can get a bit noisy at times, but she takes steps to avoid disturbing her colleagues' classrooms. Ultimately, she finds that including opportunities for discussion provides students the chance to bounce ideas off one another. In the end, students seem to learn the thinking and writing procedures better than they might accomplish by attempting the process strictly on their own.

Questions for Reflection

1. What has Sonja foregrounded in teaching the language strand of the English curriculum?

2. To what extent has her instruction helped prepare students to perform well on standardized tests?

3. In what manner, if at all, does Sonja's approach prepare her students to meet the Common Core State Standards?

4. How effectively has Sonja taught so as to provide her students with an authentic literacy experience?

5. What effects does Sonja's teaching approach have on students' ability to speak and write properly?

6. What is the likelihood that Sonja's teaching will benefit students' literacy in future English classes?

7. What is the likelihood that Sonja's teaching will help students do well academically in their courses across the high school curriculum?

8. What does Sonja overlook in deciding to teach this way, and what problems might follow from her decision to teach language literacy in this manner?

9. If you were evaluating her as an administrator, how would you assess her teaching?

SCENARIO 2: The Literature Strand of the Language Arts Curriculum

The setting: The community of Maple Heights sits on the edge of a major metropolitan area and hosts two high schools, Maple Heights Central and Maple Heights North. Central is the original community high school and, in the minds of many, the community's more beloved institution. North was built in 1980 to accommodate growth and is still viewed as the city's second school. It serves many of the newer residents, who typically are of working class origins, along with those more affluent students who are not included in Central's feeder district. Central's students annually outperform North's students on every testing measure, leading many residents to write frequently to the city's weekly newspaper complaining about the poor teaching at North, questioning the investment of funds in a low-performing school, criticizing the students' lack of commitment to their education, claiming that the students' parents are not raising their kids properly, and questioning the value of the school to the community's real estate values.

The characters: Fifteen-year veteran tenth-grade English teacher Brooke Martinez and her students at Maple Heights North High School.

The context: Brooke works amidst disagreements about the content of the literature curriculum and how to teach it, including the following factors:

- The district English curriculum has not changed substantially since the 1950s, when the community had one demographically homogeneous population. It is built around the study of canonical works. In the tenth grade, the students read Shakespeare's *Julius Caesar,* Homer's *The Odyssey,* Knowles's *A Separate Peace,* and other classic texts.
- Principal Dale Anderson used to be an English teacher at Maple Heights Central, where he taught AP and honors English. He wrote his master's thesis in English literature on the pastoral influences on Nathaniel Hawthorne's *The Marble Faun,* passing with distinction. At Central he founded the Maple Heights Literary Society, a group of teachers who met each month to discuss a master work from a list generated by a Great Books program. Principle Anderson had hoped to replicate this club at Maple Heights North but could not recruit enough interested faculty for it to work.
- Principal Anderson's favorite subject is American Literature, and he annually teaches an honors class for juniors. He also takes an interest in the junior year English curriculum, making sure that it is taught according to canonical traditions so that students primarily read nineteenth- and twentieth-century authors. He expects the sophomore English teachers to prepare students so that they are ready for a year of writing analytic essays on this literature. By the end of their junior year, he believes, students should be proficient at producing interpretations aligned with those of the critical masters, so that they are ready for the rigors of senior year English, which involves studying British Literature. This preparation will in turn, he tells his faculty, give North's students an advantage in their college English courses.
- Several of Brooke's students are part of a spoken word collaborative that meets in a community center. The group once applied for status as a school club so that they would meet conveniently after school, but the application was denied because Principal Anderson was concerned about the possibility of misogyny, violence, illegal activities, and profanity being practiced and promoted on school grounds.
- A parents' group, Literacy for New Heights, continually pressures the school to reconsider its emphasis on classic literature when too many students have more fundamental literacy needs. On their website and in letters to the city newspaper,

they ask why English is required for four years when it is focused on reading old stories, which, they argue, students will never need once they leave school. If English is to be a required course taken every year in school, they maintain, it needs to serve a basic learning need. They assert that analyzing stories is not such a need, particularly compared with the value of more basic reading and writing skills, which students can use in other classes, in college, and in jobs.

- Dinah Washington, Brooke's colleague in the English department, has written several articles published in academic journals in which she argues that the print medium is an obsolete way of thinking about texts. According to Washington, literature is just one type of text, and books are twentieth-century—rather than twenty-first-century—platforms for reading. She uses film, graphic novels, digital media, and a variety of "smart" technology tools in her classroom to prepare her students for the electronic, multimedia world that awaits them following graduation. On her blog, she implies that most educators are hopelessly outdated and will be viewed as irrelevant to students who live in the fast-paced digital world—unless they adapt to her way of teaching.

- To address the school's poor performance on the verbal portion of standardized tests, Superintendant Liz Reynolds is requiring all teachers in subjects that are tested to spend at least one week each month providing students with test preparation instruction.

The dilemma: Brooke hopes to teach her classes so that her students meet both traditional and contemporary standards for literary learning as a literacy skill. Literature represents one of the three curriculum strands, although in reality it occupies far more than one-third of her instructional time. She feels herself pulled in many seemingly opposite directions by

- Principal Anderson's reliance on the cultural heritage tradition;
- the parents' concern for literacy instruction that serves the kids beyond literary study;
- the seductive possibilities afforded by new digital literacy tools; and
- the need for her school to look better in the eyes of the community by having students score higher on standardized tests.

She thus needs to find a way of teaching the literature curriculum so that she can satisfy multiple goals with one general approach, and at the same time pacify multiple stakeholders.

The "solution": Brooke decides to organize the sophomore year literature curriculum according to a series of themes. She first considers which themes would be developmentally appropriate for her students, who are fifteen or sixteen years old, and decides that each theme will explore some sort of adolescent dilemma or other relevant archetype that is aligned with the required reading list. She plans to spend four or five weeks on each theme and organizes the students' reading into the following units:

- Coming of Age
- Loyalty
- Conflict With Authority
- Personal Identity in Social Context
- The Heroic Journey
- Peer Pressure and Social Groups
- Loss of Innocence
- Bullying

She understands that she might need to modify these selections to account for time dedicated to test preparation, test taking, pep rallies, school assemblies, snow days, bees flying in the classroom windows, and other interruptions to her planned instruction.

For each unit, she tries to include both literature and other kinds of reading. In the unit on Conflict With Authority, for instance, students read both news stories and personal accounts available on the Internet about teenagers' conflicts with authority figures. Their literary reading includes a series of short stories from the required anthology, including James Baldwin's "The Man Child," Willa Cather's "The Sentimentality of William Tavener," Bordon Deal's "Antaeus," Daphne du Maurier's "The Old Man," Simon Ortiz's "Woman Singing," and Kurt Vonnegut's "Harrison Bergeron." This preparation leads to their reading of the unit's major work, George Orwell's *Animal Farm.* Their writing includes a variety of ways of exploring the topic, including the option to keep a personal journal or blog for extra credit, a personal experience narrative about a conflict with authority, and creative opportunities such as dramatizing their personal experience narratives as a class performance, accompanied by both a written script and a dramatic storyboard. The dramatization can optionally be video-recorded and shown on a screen or uploaded to the class website and social media page.

In addition to building her instruction in writing into the unit theme, Brooke includes attention to the language strand. Because writing about conflicts might involve using a syntax that allows for contrasts (e.g., "My father wanted me to cut the grass; however, I had other plans."), she includes instruction in conjunctive adverbs. To do so, she develops a set of paired clauses that provide contrasts, such as "I wanted to date Ryan" and "My mother said I couldn't." Students then use conjunctive adverbs to connect them in sentences such as, "I wanted to date Ryan; nonetheless, my mother said I couldn't." Students are required to include at least one such construction in their personal narratives on their conflicts with authority.

The rationale for the instruction: Brooke's decision to teach according to themes reveals her value on literary meaning. Literary themes, she believes, enable students to read their own worlds of experience into the texts. By studying a particular theme across particular texts, students are able to develop a richer understanding of both the texts and their own related experiences. The English curriculum thus provides students with strategies for knowing how to read a particular type of narrative (e.g., students learn that stories about conflict with authority tend to follow a conventional structure). This approach also allows Brooke to teach English literature as a relevant topic because students can reflect on their own experiences in light of those of the characters and conflicts they read about.

Brooke's decision to provide opportunities for open-ended response is also related to the issue of relevance. She decides against explaining that each story has a conventional, authoritative interpretation because doing so might steer students away from potentially meaningful engagements of their own. Rather, she allows for journal writing in which students may explore topics without concern for being right or wrong. She finds that some of the students stray from the source, but many do stay on track. Writing personal narratives in relation to their reading engages students with the genre under study, and it meets the curricular demand of including narrative writing during the year.

With this approach, Brooke effectively ties the literary study to the writing strand in a logical way. She also includes language study by providing attention to a particular syntactic structure that often comes into play when writing about conflicts. She finds that this mode of curricular integration efficiently synthesizes literature, writing, and language instruction with one stroke. Moreover, her teaching in each area elevates the students' performance in the other two strands.

Questions for Reflection

1. What has Brooke foregrounded in teaching the literature strand of the English curriculum?

2. To what extent has her instruction helped prepare students to perform well on standardized tests?

3. In what manner, if at all, does Brooke's approach prepare her students to meet the Common Core State Standards?

4. How effectively has Brooke taught so as to provide her students with an authentic literacy experience?

5. What effects will Brooke's teaching approach have on students' ability to read literature with understanding on future occasions?

6. What is the likelihood that Brooke's teaching will benefit students' literacy performances in future English classes?

7. What is the likelihood that Brooke's teaching will help students do well academically in their courses across the high school curriculum?

8. What does Brooke overlook in deciding to teach this way, and what problems might follow from her decision to teach the literature strand in this manner?

9. If you were evaluating her as an administrator, how would you assess her teaching?

SCENARIO 3: The Writing Strand of the Language Arts Curriculum

The setting: Western Estates High School (WEHS) is located in a residential community about an hour from a metropolitan area. The town's only high school, WEHS is fed by three middle schools, and it has long held a position as a cherished community institution. Many people who settle in the district were once students at WEHS themselves and have returned to the community to raise their own children and educate them in the town's schools. The student population is relatively homogeneous, with 75 percent of the students European American and mostly middle class, 10 percent Latino/a, 10 percent African American, 3 percent Asian American, and 2 percent Native American.

The characters: English teacher Blake Hartsman and his tenth-grade students. He likes teaching at Western Estates High School and wants to live and teach in the community for the remainder of his career. Being a good citizen of the department and school is therefore an important consideration in the decisions he makes as a teacher.

The context: Blake's thinking is complicated by a number of factors, including the following:

- The state writing test is given annually to tenth-grade students, and the district's reputation is based in part on the students' performance. Further, a powerful state senator who is a resident of the town is trying to enact legislation that links teacher retention and pay to test score results. The state writing test uses a single scoring rubric for all writing genres. Regardless of the kind of writing produced, each paper must have an introductory paragraph that includes a thesis statement and a sentence explaining what each body paragraph will contain; three body paragraphs that include a topic sentence and at least one supporting example; and a conclusion that restates the paper's thesis and summarizes the key points. This rubric is used for narrative as well as persuasive and descriptive writing.
- The school curriculum on the whole is considered stable and "traditional." In English, department chair Hazel Wright, who graduated from WEHS before returning there to teach the year after graduating from the nearby state university, prefers that teachers have students read the classics along with occasional young adult novels and other stories and poems as teachers see appropriate. Although the teachers have the latitude to add material to the curriculum, on the whole, they feel comfortable with teaching from the tried-and-true anthology and having students write according to the traditional genres of narrative, description, argumentation, and research. The department also follows a historic approach to teaching writing, using a grammar and composition textbook that emphasizes correct form for whole papers, sentences, and words, and teaching students by providing models of properly formed examples.

- Blake's colleague, Suzanne Walters, recently spent part of the summer at an institute held by one of her state's National Writing Project sites. She has returned to school excited about emphasizing the process of writing rather than the form, allowing students to choose their own topics, writing personal rather than analytic papers, getting abundant peer feedback throughout the process of composing, having students generate their own grading rubrics to make their efforts more authentic, overlooking problems with mechanics and spelling in order to focus more on ideas, using new digital twenty-first-century literacies as vehicles for students' expression and ideas, and devoting far more time to in-class writing activities than the department has provided in the past.
- The president of the school board is the former football coach and athletic director. He believes in efficiency, and so he urges teachers to dispense with what he considers frivolities, such as writing. His priority is to make sure that students know course content through their performance on drills and multiple-choice tests, which in turn prepare them for the standardized tests that help set the real estate values in his community.
- The relatively small Native American population is led by an activist resident, Ned Barnes, who attends many school board meetings to complain that the curriculum is too oriented to language, especially writing. Many Native Americans, he asserts, distrust writing because it was the medium of broken treaties. As a result, they reject writing as the means by which they produce compacts, including writing for school. He is now considering suing the school for requiring all students to write for academic evaluation.

The dilemma: Blake needs to figure out how to teach writing within these conflicting values. He has to make sure that he

- teaches the content of the curriculum, which requires steady progress through the literature anthology;
- attends to matters of form so as to send students to their eleventh-grade teachers with the requisite understanding of proper language usage, sentence structure, and whole-text form;
- incorporates as many ideas from his knowledge of writing process as possible within the department's orientation to form; and
- teaches so that his students perform well on the standardized tests that are of major importance to his principal and colleagues, as well as to the parents of his students.

The "solution": The sophomore English curriculum is organized according to formal genres: the short story, the novel, poetry, drama, and prose. Although Blake is not convinced that teaching each of these genres for six or so weeks is best for either promoting student interest or learning how to teach each genre, he does not want to depart too radically from the department's customary ways of teaching. He decides to approach each genre strategically, providing his students with procedures for learning to figure out a text's meaning based on its structure and elements. He also plans to integrate language and writing instruction with the genre analysis so that students engage with all of the curricular strands during each unit of study.

For the unit on poetry, for instance, Blake identifies four key areas of strategic reading that help readers interpret poetic meaning:

- Understanding word connotations
- Interpreting images
- Interpreting metaphors
- Interpreting symbols

He creates a routine for approaching each strategy so that each of five consecutive weeks involves a similar structure.

As preparation for class, he reads through the literature anthology and identifies poems that require each of the strategies. He then dedicates one week to each strategy. First he leads the class through the reading of a poem in which the target strategy of understanding word connotations helps to produce an informed meaning. Part of this demonstration includes "thinking aloud" as he goes through the process of looking at the connotations of key words in the poem and then orchestrating the various connotations into an interpretive theme. He then has students work in small groups to practice the strategy with a second, unfamiliar poem. Each group is required to outline an interpretation that employs the five-paragraph template that will ultimately serve as the basis for the state writing test. Their outline consists of a thesis statement that explains the general manner in which the words' connotations shade the poem's meaning; three topic sentences for separate paragraphs that show the poet's use of the element in the poem and are supported by an example; and a concluding statement that explains the overall meaning of the poem as determined through an analysis of word connotation.

Groups share their responses with the class and get feedback. Each group then goes through the same routine with a new poem, this time providing a more detailed outline that expands on the introductory paragraph's thesis statement, explains more thoroughly why the examples illustrate the topic sentences, and provides a more nuanced understanding of the poem's meaning. This time, groups exchange their drafts and critique one another's interpretations before returning them and engaging in a whole-class discussion of both the poem's meaning and how to write five-paragraph themes interpreting it.

Blake then assigns the groups a third poem that they must analyze and that will become the basis for a full five-paragraph theme. Blake reasons that by coauthoring the essay, students will get support and feedback as they compose, which he hopes will improve their ultimate individual performances. Once again the groups exchange papers and critique one another's work, this time moving beyond the quality of the interpretation to also focus on the full range of writing expectations: paragraph form, use of topic sentences and supporting examples tied together with explanations of why the examples illustrate the claim, proper mechanics and usage, and sentence structure. Again, Blake leads a concluding discussion of the role of connotation in helping to produce the poem's meaning.

Blake goes through a similar sequence for each of the remaining strategies related to images, metaphors, and symbols. Beginning with the third week, on metaphor, he has students write individual papers rather than group papers for the week's final assignment. After spending four weeks in this manner, he takes a fifth week to focus students' move toward independent interpretation. He begins by giving them a new poem without providing prior information on which strategies are central to its interpretation. Students work in groups to identify which elements are involved and how they contribute to the poem's meaning, and they collaboratively write a five-paragraph theme interpreting it. They exchange papers with other groups for critical feedback on both their essay skills and their interpretive work, and then have an opportunity to revise the essays, which they turn in to Blake for his response. He repeats this stage of the instruction with another new poem to provide another round of practice and feedback. For the final grade of the unit, he distributes a new poem in class, one that includes each of the four elements studied in prior lessons and activities, and has each student analyze it individually and write an interpretive essay for a grade.

The rationale for the instruction: Blake's teaching attempts to provide instruction in both interpretive and writing process while also attending to issues of form in both the poetry being studied and the students' five-paragraph analytic themes. He thus tries to meet the standards of his school and department while also teaching procedures that students may apply to new reading and writing experiences.

His teaching relies on his understanding of "instructional scaffolding." This approach involves strong instructional support in the early stages of instruction that is gradually withdrawn as students demonstrate the competency to work more independently. He begins by providing a demonstration that illustrates an interpretive process through his modeling of how to think while reading a poem, and then having students use this process with peer support in their small-group sessions. Although some of his colleagues do not view this stage as writing instruction, Blake believes that it teaches students how to do the kind of *thinking* that will inform their writing, and thus, it should be considered instruction in both poetic reading and analytic writing.

The sequence of going from teacher-led modeling to small-group application of strategies to independent thinking and writing works at two levels. First, students' procedural knowledge is scaffolded as they study each of the four literary devices. Second, their knowledge increases over the course of the four episodes so that their strategies for analyzing poems build toward a robust set of interpretive skills. These skills are simultaneously built into the students' developing understanding of how to compose a five-paragraph theme, on which they will be evaluated in high-stakes tests that reflect on them, their teacher, and their school. These skills are built over the course of the instruction as students gradually assume control of their interpretive and writing abilities.

Questions for Reflection

1. What has Blake foregrounded in teaching the writing strand of the English curriculum?

2. To what extent has his instruction helped prepare students to perform well on standardized tests?

3. In what manner, if at all, does Blake's approach prepare his students to meet the Common Core State Standards?

4. How effectively has Blake taught so as to provide his students with an authentic literacy experience?

5. What effects will Blake's teaching approach have on students' ability to read literature with understanding on future occasions?

6. What is the likelihood that Blake's teaching will benefit students' literacy performances in future English classes?

7. What is the likelihood that Blake's teaching will help students do well academically in their courses across the high school curriculum?

8. What does Blake overlook in deciding to teach this way, and what problems might follow from his decision to teach the writing strand in this manner?

9. If you were evaluating him as an administrator, how would you assess his teaching?

SCENARIO 4: Promoting Literacy Through the Use of a Variety of Textual Forms

The setting: Woodyard Middle School, which is located in a suburban school district and is one of eight different middle schools that feed into the local high school. Like most schools in the area, Woodyard Middle School had aligned its curriculum with the state standards that had been in existence for more than fifteen years. However, during the past year, administrators from all eight middle schools worked with the local high school to develop a professional development plan that would serve to articulate a coherent curriculum using the Common Core State Standards (CCSS) as the foundation.

The characters: Sarah Kally, a Language Arts teacher, has been working with five other teachers. As part of the consortium-wide articulation to revise the curriculum to align with the newly adopted CCSS, all of the teachers recently attended several days of professional development. During this period, the teachers collaborated to review the standards, to decide which standards were of the greatest importance, and to begin discussing how they could collectively assess student learning in relation to the standards. As part of her training, Sarah got to analyze some experimental assessments that were created in other states as a response to the CCSS. The general belief was that the new assessments aligned with the CCSS would call upon students to analyze texts of various types, synthesize these texts in some way, and develop a thoughtful and reasonable argument in response to an authentic problem.

The context: The newly adopted standards, and the consortium-wide pressure to align curriculum with the new standards, have presented a host of new challenges for Sarah and her colleagues. But the prospect of wrestling with a new set of standards is not the only thing on Sarah's mind. Sarah's principal recently announced that all teachers at Woodyard will begin working within a professional learning community (PLC) model. The teachers at Woodyard have been operating on grade-level teams for some time, but the new PLC initiative will require them to develop ways to collect evidence of student learning in relation to specified learning targets, and to use this evidence of student learning both to influence instructional decisions and to frame student interventions.

The dilemma: Sarah and her colleagues determine that they are already on board in terms of the language standards represented in the CCSS writing instruction, because they have always emphasized grammar as a means of promoting better writing. However, they also recognize that several of the standards contain approaches that are not in alignment with their current practices. It appears that they will need to drastically change certain aspects of their instructional program to meet the new demands. For instance, very rarely, if ever, have Sarah and her colleagues used texts other than those in the adopted textbook to promote literacy learning in the classroom.

Specifically, Sarah and her colleagues must figure out how to achieve the following:

- Address the distinction that the standards create between literary texts and informational texts. To date, Sarah and the other teachers at Woodyard have typically addressed reading in a similar fashion, regardless of the type of reading their students are asked to do. Traditionally, Language Arts classes at Woodyard have provided students with exposure to various examples of literature and poetry as a means of improving their reading. None of these teachers has ever used informational texts to a great extent, and many teachers wonder why persuasive and reflective essays such as Henry David Thoreau's "Civil Disobedience" are classified as "informational."
- Determine how to teach learners to "integrate information presented in different media or formats as well as in words to develop a coherent understanding of a topic or issue" as required by CCSS RI.6.7.
- Create lessons that teach students to "compare and contrast a text to an audio, video, or multimedia version of the text, analyzing each medium's portrayal of the subject (for example, how the delivery of a speech affects the impact of the words)" (CCSS RI.7.7).
- Find ways to teach students to "analyze the representation of a subject or a key scene into different artistic mediums, including what is emphasized or absent in each treatment" (CCSS RL.9–10.7).

- Determine how to meet the demands centered on the emphasis of argumentation in the standards. Sarah is used to assigning her students expository and persuasive essays, and every now and then she takes her class to the library to research the background of an author they are reading, but to this point her teaching focus has been on the five-paragraph essay format, which has been part of the statewide assessment.

The "solution": Although Sarah and her colleagues initially viewed the movement to a PLC with suspicion, ultimately they find the ability to work together invigorating. Soon they begin relying on each other to find ways to accommodate the new standards, and working together becomes an invaluable aspect of this process. Together, Sarah and her colleagues review and analyze a variety of texts to find those that will help them adjust to the new CCSS emphasis on literary and informational texts. Sarah is able to rely on her colleagues to expand her understanding of text to include a variety of different textual forms.

Eighth graders at Woodyard all read Sandra Cisneros's *House on Mango Street.* The teachers decide to emphasize literary themes related to sense of place and belonging, and to give students supplementary readings from local and national newspapers that accentuate these themes. Students demonstrate their abilities to make direct connections between the literary and informational texts in ways that Sarah and her colleagues have not envisioned before. Sarah finds that the key to helping students make these connections is to explicitly break down the learning standard being applied and to provide students with language about literacy development that will enhance their ability to read with greater comprehension. The standards note that students have to "analyze" and "compare and contrast," but Sarah and her colleagues recognize that such high-level skills are more easily stated than accomplished. Consequently, Sarah and her colleagues work to break each CCSS reading standard into a manageable body of explicit learning targets that students can use to engage in the reading process more thoughtfully.

To their surprise, Sarah and the other members of her team find that the CCSS's emphasis on using other texts, especially nonprint texts, is a key to ensuring that the standards are being met. Sarah and her team share research articles on this topic and discuss the importance of expanding the idea of text to go beyond print and to include just about anything from which a student can derive meaning. They are particularly impressed by articles and published lesson plans that demonstrate how teachers can use images, video clips, and statistical data sets to enhance a student's ability to draw high-level inferences, thus giving students practice with a skill that has the potential to improve their ability to draw inferences in other reading situations.

Using a breakdown of reading skills as suggested by the standards, Sarah learns to help her students approach the act of reading in a more metacognitive fashion. Sarah and her colleagues find that both the CCSS and the College Readiness Standards articulate a hierarchy of reading comprehension that begins with understanding a text at its most basic stated level and then builds to generating more complex inferences based on key details or features of the text. Sarah relies on her previous exposure to this taxonomical view of reading, which occurred during a methods and materials class she took during her teacher preparation. Sarah and the other teachers develop materials that give students explicit practice in understanding the various levels of comprehension employed during the process of reading, and then they work to give students exposure to this recursive process using a variety of texts, especially the type of nonprint texts indicated within the CCSS. Sarah finds that her students are able to transfer the skills they practice with less traditional texts to other reading tasks.

Sarah becomes increasingly fond of a particular strategy that involves pairing a literary or nonfiction text with an image, like a painting, and asking students to work their way through the hierarchy of reading strategies that they consistently practice with other texts to help develop a more nuanced level of comprehension. Sarah enjoys using famous works of art, especially realistic paintings, to help students become familiar with the practice of pointing out key details that lead to a more overarching statement of theme or purpose related to the text. In one lesson, Sarah has her class analyze a series of portraits of homeless people. The class identifies specific aspects of the portraits that suggest bigger ideas to them. They use these details to defend generalizations about character and theme and then reflect on these ideas further while reading an article about homelessness from a national publication. Throughout all of these applications, Sarah presses her students to

- reflect on the means by which they are establishing an understanding of basic ideas and key details, and
- note how they are collecting these ideas and connecting the dots of these details to draw more complex and interesting inferences.

Sarah continually provides her students with explicit feedback about the success they are having with these foundational reading skills, and students build on this feedback as the texts that Sarah selects become more rigorous and complex.

The rationale for the instruction: Sarah and her colleagues worked within the required framework to work toward solutions to challenges that they had been facing all along, yet which required special attention in the context of the CCSS adoption. They used the professional learning communities as a way to collaborate on troubleshooting and problem solving, drawing on one another's knowledge, experience, and expertise to address school-specific issues in the context of the larger mandate.

Although she and her colleagues might have also appreciated and encouraged such experiences as their students' emotional engagement with reading, they found value in the more technical strategic emphasis of the CCSS. This attention led to a consideration of how to teach the reading and literature strand of the curriculum in terms of metacognition so that students could "learn to learn" how to read not just the text in front of them, but later texts built on similar formal structures and calling for similar interpretive strategies.

She got around the possible problem of making reading a dry, technical experience by having her students learn to draw inferences about critical social problems in which they had an emotional commitment, such as homelessness. As a result, she was able to work within the CCSS directives without abandoning her belief that reading can help her students become better people and make a positive mark on society through careful analysis of social problems, heartfelt engagement with issues, and reflection on their thought processes.

Questions for Reflection

1. What has Sarah foregrounded in teaching the language strand of the English curriculum?

2. To what extent has her instruction helped prepare students to perform well on standardized tests?

3. In what manner, if at all, does Sarah's approach prepare her students to meet the Common Core State Standards?

4. How effectively has Sarah taught so as to provide her students with an authentic literacy experience?

5. What effects will Sarah's teaching approach have on students' ability to speak and write properly on future occasions?

6. What is the likelihood that Sarah's teaching will benefit students' literacy in future English classes?

7. What is the likelihood that Sarah's teaching will help students do well academically in their courses across the high school curriculum?

8. What does Sarah overlook in deciding to teach this way, and what problems might follow from her decision to teach language literacy in this manner?

9. If you were evaluating her as an administrator, how would you assess her teaching?

SCENARIO 5: Developing Literacy in a Technological Age

The setting: Roosevelt High School, an urban high school that serves just over three thousand students.

The characters: Akash Shima has been an English teacher for ten years at Roosevelt High. He teaches three sections of regular junior English and two sections of World Masterpieces, an accelerated senior elective that attracts high-performing students who choose not to take Advance Placement senior English.

The context: Akash has become increasingly frustrated. It appears that some students are reluctant to do their assigned reading, and others are simply refusing to do it. Akash is relatively sure that *he* is not the problem, because his colleagues also complain about how their students are not reading. In fact, many are quick to characterize today's students as lazy and increasingly complacent. Akash disagrees with this assessment, and lately he has been wondering if the reading issue is centered on students' increasing reliance on and exposure to technology. With so many diversions, perhaps students are finding it difficult to focus on the print medium with which his generation had grown up.

As is the case at many schools around the nation, Akash and his colleagues at Roosevelt High School have also been concerned with the impact of the recently adopted CCSS. This apprehension is even greater for schools like Roosevelt, and for other schools throughout the state, because each school stands to receive a great deal of grant money that will be awarded by virtue of the state's status as one of the winners in the federal government's "Race to the Top" initiative. Like all schools throughout the state, Roosevelt had contributed to the state's eligibility for the award by committing to adopting the CCSS quickly as well as to adopting the assessment protocols that accompany the CCSS. Akash and his colleagues have found that committing to the standards was one thing, but establishing the means by which to develop instruction and assessment around the standards is something else entirely.

The dilemma: Akash knows that to integrate the CCSS into his existing practice, he will need to address several challenges.

- He will need to engage students in reading so that they recognize the value of and choose to complete the assignments.
- He will need to ensure that the reading material is challenging enough. A consultant from the U.S. Department of Education, who visited Roosevelt to announce the news of the school's award, had shared several insights about the CCSS and their intended impact. The consultant noted that the CCSS places an emphasis on reading more complex texts, and as a means of illustrating the point, shared published and lengthy lists of exemplar texts to help guide teachers in text selection. Akash recalls the queasy feeling in his stomach when he reviewed the list of Grade 11 text exemplars and saw *The Canterbury Tales*, *Pride and Prejudice*, *Jane Eyre*, *Hamlet*, and *Their Eyes Were Watching God*, a list that included titles that he felt very few of his students would or could read, along with titles that did not fit with the American Literature emphasis of eleventh grade. They would much prefer, he feels, the sort of YAL novels that his school had begun gravitating toward before the adoption of the CCSS.
- He will need to help students learn to interpret text independently. The consultant also noted that whereas teachers in high school tend to scaffold and support students during the reading of a text, colleges expect students to read more independently.
- He will need to take steps to include more informational reading. The consultant explained that the CCSS assert the importance of reading in all disciplines.

They further require that 70 percent of high school reading requirements center on informational reading, leaving him to wonder how to approach such texts as Patrick Henry's "Speech to the Virginia Convention" and Jonathan Swift's "A Modest Proposal," neither of which he considers either fictional or informational.

- The stipulation of predominantly "informational" texts suggests to most who implement CCSS the need to teach reading far beyond the four walls of English classrooms. Akash recognizes that with the promise of reading standards in Social Science and Science in upcoming years, the prospect of teaching reading in all the disciplines is becoming a clear expectation.

The "solution": To address these challenges, Akash and his colleagues root their instruction in some common principles that help them forge a coherent framework of instruction that addresses their concerns. The department works to avoid stereotyping and characterization (e.g., viewing students as lazy), which does little to enhance the manner in which they engage students in learning. They recognize that although it may be increasingly common—and easy—to bemoan the current state of affairs and lament the "impossible" task of engaging "screenagers" in reading and helping them develop as readers, it is much more productive to focus on the growth they can help students realize. They conclude that although students today have access to technology that had been unimaginable only a few years before, the challenge of reaching today's students is no greater than the challenge of engaging students in prior generations who faced different, but no less significant, challenges.

Akash and his colleagues work to establish a foundational approach to literacy instruction that emphasizes the development of background knowledge that can help students establish a clear purpose for their reading. This focus also helps students become more motivated to do their reading. Akash and his colleagues reflect on how they can approach literacy instruction more holistically, and this consideration leads to a study about developing their curriculum around specific inquiry frames that will help to engage students in their learning more deeply.

The English teachers at Roosevelt work together to refashion the curriculum around a series of essential questions that can guide student reading and motivate students to read with greater purpose and enthusiasm. For instance, whereas Akash's World Masterpiece class previously centered on a traditional framework that exposed students to literary movements like Romanticism and Transcendentalism, teachers have now reworked units in a way that encourages students to pursue more complex responses to essential questions, such as, "Just because scientists can do something, does that mean that they should do it?" and "What are the costs to a society that fails to promote equality?" Akash finds that his students are far more prone to read when he is able to position the reading within an inquiry frame that students find relevant.

The inquiry approach devised by Akash and his colleagues is assisted by a new emphasis on classroom dialogue and discussion. In addition to posing essential questions as a means of engaging in and reflecting on their reading, Akash finds that providing students the opportunity to wrestle with these questions in discussion during class allows them to develop and refine their thinking in ways they could not do before when Akash did most of the talking in class from the front of the classroom.

Learning to structure classroom discussions carefully has not been easy, and some days are better than others. However, Akash sees the emphasis on getting students to talk more in class as a valuable contribution to his mission to get more of his students reading. Seeking to get his students more personally involved in the process of providing feedback from class experiences, Akash now asks students routinely about the extent to which the classroom discussions are enhancing their reading experience. An overwhelming majority of students consistently respond that they find the prospect of coming to class to share their responses to their reading with their peers as a significant factor in their motivation for completing their assigned reading. Akash has also discovered additional value in having students use the result of classroom discussions in their writing assignments. By elevating classroom discussion to the point where it receives the same treatment as the published books the students read, Akash is able to motivate students even more.

As Akash and his colleagues research more about promoting a culture of readers, they also begin to relinquish some of the control of the reading content of their instructional program. Now Akash employs more reading choice. While courses such as World Masterpieces still emphasize canonical texts—The Epic of Gilgamesh, Hamlet, Frankenstein, and their classical kin—Akash and his colleagues now employ literature circles and other classroom activities that allow students to choose books that they can then bring in and relate to other aspects of classroom inquiry that are nurtured in class each day.

Akash and other English teachers at Roosevelt further realize the draw that technology plays in the lives of their students. They begin to incorporate technology in their classrooms whenever they can. With the benefit of some of their "Race to the Top" funding, the teachers have access to document cameras and digital projectors that allow them to easily share student responses to essential questions, a practice that helps push classroom conversations in new and interesting directions. The teachers share an electronic tablet cart secured with grant money, and they have learned to use the devices in ways that tap into students' latent appreciation for technology-based learning opportunities that are also linked with classroom inquiry.

For instance, in one lesson, Akash works with his students to develop dialogue for the narratives they are writing. He has his students use a messaging application on the tablets to engage in a virtual discussion about a hypothetical case study that depicts a principal who takes some unpopular measures to address what he feels is inappropriate dancing during school-sponsored events. Using the messaging program, students engage in a back-and-forth dialogue about the situation and later convert the exchanges they create into dialogue for their narratives. It takes students some time to get over the fact that they are texting in class, but they begin to work immediately and see how the application of a technology-based dialogue form to which they had become so acclimated could be used in a new way to enhance their learning.

By adapting their teaching and adopting an "If you can't beat 'em, join 'em" philosophy, Akash Shima and his colleagues at Roosevelt High School are able to transform their own thinking about the role of reading in a technological age, which, in turn, helps them transform the culture of reading at their school.

The rationale for the instruction: Akash and his colleagues avoided a common tendency among adults, which is to dismiss kids who feel schoolwork is tedious as lazy and unmotivated. His challenge instead was to provide a setting in which more motivated reading became available. That is, rather than locating "motivation" as an intrinsic problem of individual people, he considered himself as responsible to an extent for constructing a motivating environment that was attentive to his students' life stages in their human development and the interests that, outside school, motivated them to become engaged.

The development of compelling essential questions around which to organize the curriculum served as a central dimension of that environment, providing them with goals toward which to direct their inquiries and considering the range of texts through which those inquiries might be conducted. In addition to appropriate texts, he considered which tools might most appropriately enable the students to work with alacrity, precision, and depth. The affordance of digital media tools thus both brought students' chosen media into the classroom and gave them more sophisticated problems toward which to apply them.

Ultimately, these tools served both personal and academic ends as the students constructed narratives that both expressed their beliefs about the world and prepared them for the assessments that accompanied the new curriculum.

Questions for Reflection

1. What has Akash foregrounded in teaching the language strand of the English curriculum?

2. To what extent has his instruction helped prepare students to perform well on standardized tests?

3. In what manner, if at all, does Akash's approach prepare his students to meet the Common Core State Standards?

4. How effectively has Akash taught so as to provide his students with an authentic literacy experience?

5. What effects will Akash's teaching approach have on students' ability to speak and write properly on future occasions?

6. What is the likelihood that Akash's teaching will benefit students' literacy in future English classes?

7. What is the likelihood that Akash's teaching will help students do well academically in their courses across the high school curriculum?

8. What does Akash overlook in deciding to teach this way, and what problems might follow from his decision to teach language literacy in this manner?

9. If you were evaluating him as an administrator, how would you assess his teaching?

REFERENCES

Alim, H. S., & Baugh, J. (Eds.). (2006). *Talkin Black talk: Language, education, and social change.* New York, NY: Teachers College Press.

Applebee, A. N. (1993). *Literature in the secondary school: Studies of curriculum and instruction in the United States* (NCTE Research Report No. 25). Urbana, IL: National Council of Teachers of English.

Beach, R. (1993). *A teacher's introduction to reader-response theories.* Urbana, IL: National Council of Teachers of English.

Hicks, T. (2013). *Crafting digital writing: Composing texts across media and genres.* Portsmouth, NH: Heinemann.

Hillocks, G. (1986). *Research on written composition: New directions for teaching.* Urbana, IL: ERIC Clearinghouse on Reading and Communications Skills and National Conference on Research in English.

Hillocks, G. (2002). *The testing trap: How state writing assessments control learning.* New York, NY: Teachers College Press.

Johnson, T. S., Smagorinsky, P., Thompson, L., & Fry, P. G. (2003). Learning to teach the five-paragraph theme. *Research in the Teaching of English, 38,* 136–176. Retrieved from http://www.petersmagorinsky.net/About/PDF/RTE/RTE2003.pdf

Kinloch, V. (2010). *Harlem on our minds: Place, race, and the literacies of urban youth.* New York, NY: Teachers College Press.

Smagorinsky, P., Johannessen, L. R., Kahn, E. A., & McCann, T. M. (2010). *The dynamics of writing instruction: A structured process approach for middle and high school.* Portsmouth, NH: Heinemann.

Weaver, C. (1996). *Teaching grammar in context.* Portsmouth, NH: Heinemann.

2 Toward Disciplinary Reading and Writing in History

Chauncey Monte-Sano and Denise Miles

The Common Core State Standards (Council of Chief State School Officers, 2010) directly integrate reading and writing into history and social studies. Students are expected to write informative text, narratives, and arguments, and to comprehend, analyze, and evaluate information while reading. The latest social studies document, the College, Career, and Civic Life C3 Framework for Social Studies State Standards (National Council for the Social Studies [NCSS], 2013), frames social studies as an inquiry process in which reading and analysis of historical sources, argumentation, constructing conclusions, and communicating them, are paramount. Yet, based on results from the National Assessment of Educational Progress (NAEP), only 29 percent of eighth graders have appropriate grade-level skills in reading and writing (National Center for Educational Statistics [NCES], 2007, 2008). Only 2 percent of eighth graders tested in reading could interpret an author's purpose as expressed in a text or use examples to explain their conclusions about a text (NCES, 2007). As for writing, only 2 percent of twelfth graders tested could claim a position and consistently support it with well-chosen reasons and examples (NCES,

2008). Further, most states require teachers to cover the information included in dense state standards documents and test students on their knowledge of this array of information. How is literacy to be taught in history and social studies given such challenges? This chapter will review research on students' reading, thinking, and writing in history and approaches to teaching that help students develop literacy practices rooted in the discipline as they also learn content knowledge.

WHAT IS THE ROLE OF LITERACY IN HISTORY?

This chapter approaches history as evidence-based interpretation in which inquiry is central. The inquiry process involves working with and interrogating historical artifacts in an effort to understand and explain the past. Such a process includes analyzing evidence, interpreting the meaning of evidence, and using evidence to construct and explain historically plausible accounts of the past. Historians typically express these accounts as written arguments. Historical ways of thinking (referred to as "disciplinary concepts and tools" in the C3 Framework) are embedded in the processes of reading, analysis, and interpretation; in other words, historical thinking facilitates historical literacy practices. For example, the C3 Framework highlights concepts and tools such as change, continuity, context, perspective, sources, evidence, and causation (NCSS, 2013).

Because a disciplinary approach to history privileges analysis and interpretation of historical texts, it naturally emphasizes reading, writing, and thinking. For example, historians analyze evidence, weigh conflicting accounts, consider the influence of bias, and develop evidence-based arguments. All of this thinking is embedded in reading and writing practices. Reading is a key to analysis and constructing interpretations of the past. Writing is a key to conveying that interpretation to others in the field and is often integrated into the thinking process that develops the interpretation (e.g., writing marginal notes next to a historical document or writing outlines).

READING HISTORY

Goals for reading history. Because the goal of historical interpretation is to understand the past, historical reasoning involves reading evidence from the perspective of those who created it and putting it into context. Historians can only interrogate artifacts from the past since the events under study cannot be repeated: Typically, historians have not witnessed the events about which they write, and the authors of the documents they use to analyze the past are inaccessible (cf. Hexter, 1971). In order to understand why something happened in the past or what compelled someone to create a particular text (whether written or visual), historians must situate authors and events in the context of contemporary events, peers, and ideas; such an approach to reading highlights the relationships between contiguous events (cf. Mink, 1987).

Particular approaches to reading historical sources facilitate the historical reasoning process. As Wineburg (2001) found, historians source, corroborate, and contextualize evidence as they read and make sense of the past. Sourcing involves noting authors of historical documents as well as their intentions and assumptions. Contextualization includes situating a historical document in the time and place in which it was created. Corroboration involves comparing multiple historical documents to facilitate sense making and determine acceptable facts. Wineburg argued that historical texts are excerpts of social situations; those situations—including the actors and their contexts—must be re-created so that readers more fully understand the texts themselves. Historians' reading focused on the position, motivation, and potential biases of the author before reading the rest of the text. Knowing the author's perspective shaped how historians weighed evidence and developed their own interpretations. The iterative process of moving between these kinds of questions and evidence eventually leads historians to make a case for a particular interpretation of the past.

Students' tendencies in reading history. However, students do not naturally tend to read like historians (Wineburg, 2001). In reading historical texts, they often focus on the literal meaning of documents and miss intertextual reading strategies that would promote interpretive work (e.g., Afflerbach & VanSledright, 2001). In one study of reading multiple texts, students were unlikely to notice source information unless explicitly instructed to do so (Britt & Aglinskas, 2002). Research also confirms that students use their own background knowledge of historical topics to make sense of texts (Perfetti, Britt, & Georgi, 1995; Wolfe & Goldman, 2005), for better or worse.

A powerful example of students' tendencies in reading history comes from a student's response to a task from *Historical Thinking Matters,* a website for history educators. The task contrasts two newspaper articles about the sinking of the *USS Maine.* Both articles were published on February 17, 1898, one day after the event.[1] One article, posted in Hearst's *New York Journal and Advertiser,* is a classic example of yellow journalism in its insistence on blaming Spain as the aggressor for planting a mine in Havana harbor. In contrast, the second article, posted in the *New York Times,* quotes the secretary of the navy, who says he does not think an enemy is responsible for the explosion and also says he will wait for a full report of the explosion before he lays blame. Another part of the website shares a high school student's thinking as he read these documents.[2] The student, Matt, noticed that each said something different, but he assumed that they were by the same writer. He explained the discrepancy by saying, "I guess the next day, they're like, oh we didn't say that. Kind of interesting switch." Matt's response shows us that he is able to comprehend the documents on a basic level, but he lacks historical reading strategies such as sourcing and contextualization. As a result, he misses important clues to the meaning of the document, such as the publisher of each newspaper article and the dates on which both articles were published. Given these tendencies, how do we support students' reading?

Practices that help students read historically. Historical literacy research indicates that the kinds of texts students work with influence their reasoning processes. Bain (2006) explains well the difficulties students face when working with authoritative textbooks that don't support interpretive thinking. Rouet, Britt, Mason, and Perfetti (1996) found that when college students read primary documents, they were more likely to evaluate the genre of the document and cite passages in their writing. Students were less likely to do so when reading historians' monographs or textbooks. Paxton (2002) found that historical texts with "visible authors" increased the chances that students would interact with the texts as they read. Texts with "visible authors" included primary documents or historians' monographs; the key appeared to be that an authorial voice was clearly present. Several studies have confirmed that reading multiple texts supports students' historical thinking, although it is questionable whether more than two texts are necessary for novices (Hynd, 1999; Stahl, Hynd, Britton, McNish, & Bosquet, 1996; Wiley & Voss, 1999).

The instruction and activities that accompany reading historical documents also influence students' reading. Hynd-Shanahan, Holschuh, and Hubbard (2004) found that college students who discussed how historians read and the nature of historical texts were more able to read for historical meaning. The combination of reading multiple texts that challenge students' preconceptions and activities such as discussion or group work also appears to encourage historical thinking (Ashby, Lee, & Shemilt, 2005; Bain, 2005). When it came to multiple texts, students' beliefs about how historical knowledge is produced (Braten & Stromso, 2006) and level of disciplinary expertise (Rouet, Favart, Britt, & Perfetti, 1997) also influenced their ability to synthesize ideas across texts. Together, these studies suggest that students are more successful at historical reading when teachers

- offer tasks that represent the work of historians,
- encourage students to use multiple historical sources,
- provide sources with a clear voice, and
- promote an understanding of the discipline.

Two recent studies extend these earlier findings and build off the cognitive apprenticeship approach to instruction (Collins, Brown, & Holum, 1991). In a cognitive apprenticeship, teachers model and think aloud so that advanced thinking becomes visible. When modeling, teachers must make expertise explicit so that students can learn and improve. After modeling, teachers give students guided practice in the skills or strategies to be acquired, along with feedback to help learners improve. Finally, the students practice independently. This process leads to the development of expertise over time.

Nokes, Dole, and Hacker (2007) developed four interventions in eleventh-grade U.S. history classes that compared the use of multiple texts and textbooks as well as traditional content instruction and explicit teaching of historical reading strategies (or heuristics). After a three-week period, researchers found that students who used multiple texts scored the highest on a test of content knowledge mastery and used sourcing and corroboration more often than those who read traditional textbooks. In addition, those students who used multiple texts and received explicit instruction in historical reading strategies performed better on a test of their heuristics use. Specifically, these students sourced and corroborated significantly more on the posttest than on the pretest. Few students in any of the conditions contextualized documents.

Reisman (2012) implemented a curriculum intervention in the San Francisco Unified school district that involved explicitly teaching students the skills of historical analysis while reading documents and developing interpretations. The intervention, called Reading Like a Historian, included posters for four distinct historical reading practices: sourcing, contextualizing, close reading, and corroboration.[3] Each poster identified key questions readers ask of texts.

In addition, teachers in Reisman's study gave students historical questions with at least two relevant documents for more than seventy lessons delivered throughout the eleventh-grade U.S. history curriculum. In one example, teachers asked, "Were the Puritans selfish or selfless?" Then teachers delivered relevant background information and gave students John Winthrop's 1630 "City Upon a Hill" sermon along with John Cotton's 1630 "The Divine Right to Occupy the Land" sermon. Reisman provided additional scaffolding in the form of historical thinking questions specifically tailored to these documents. Finally, she shortened and adapted the documents so that they were appropriate to students' reading levels.[4] Reisman found that students who participated in the intervention improved on tests of historical thinking, basic reading comprehension, and retention of historical content by the end of the school year.

WRITING HISTORY

Goals for writing history. Making the case for a particular interpretation in writing is central to historical study. Argument writing encompasses key features of historical writing, and so we focus on that particular text type here. Toulmin's (1958) argumentation framework lays out aspects of writing such as claim, data, warrant, and counterargument, components that apply to most disciplines, including history. Historical writing shares an argumentation stance with other forms of writing, but the nature of the questions, data, and warrants (or the evidence and connection between evidence and claim) is discipline specific (Monte-Sano, 2012b; cf. Bazerman & Paradis, 1991). In the construction of historical arguments, writing is often inextricable from disciplinary ways of thinking and working with evidence. According to history experts, the use and framing of evidence in historical writing indicate key aspects of disciplinary reasoning, including recognizing biases in sources, comparing evidence, situating evidence in its context, and taking into account different perspectives and multiple causes (Collingwood, 1946/1993; Hexter, 1971; Mink, 1987).

Historical interpretations rely on the public display of evidence to substantiate claims: A claim cannot stand without evidence to support it (Collingwood, 1946/1993; Hexter, 1971). The inclusion of examples, details, footnotes, and quotations exemplifies this aspect of reasoning. Stating where evidence comes from (i.e., sources of quotations and information) is paramount in that it allows others to understand and evaluate the basis for the claims. Further, historical interpretations must account for the available evidence (Hexter, 1971). This reconciliation may involve altering interpretations to accommodate contradictory evidence. Comparing different—and contrasting—documents is a visible manifestation of this way of reasoning.

Students' tendencies in writing history. Writing historically is challenging. Writing evidence-based historical essays involves sifting through evidence and constructing an interpretation in writing. However, adolescents tend to see the goals of writing differently than do historians. For example, in Greene's (1994) research, college students were less likely than historians to recognize that writing involved constructing an argument and situating a topic in its historical context by connecting related issues.

Writing text-based interpretation is particularly difficult, because it entails synthesizing and organizing information to suit the writer's own purposes (for more on this, see Greene & Ackerman, 1996). In one study, college students were asked to read and interpret others' texts in order to create their own position; instead of creating original arguments, most simply summarized or shared their ideas in response to the texts they read (Flower et al., 1990). Still another challenge in historical writing is students' lack of historical language, which inhibits their ability to think in terms of another time and context (Edwards, 1978).

In terms of a writer's process, Bereiter and Scardamalia (1987) argue that nonexpert writers transfer their knowledge to the texts they write in a model known as "knowledge-telling." Nonexperts engage in a unidirectional process of first establishing a claim and then finding facts to support it (as opposed to experts who engage in a dialectical process of writing in which they move back and forth between their knowledge and their writing and thus transform the knowledge they share in writing). According to McCutchen (2006), novices may resort to knowledge-telling as a way to manage the complex demands of writing. The cognitive processes of reflection and planning, text production, revising, and text interpretation (e.g., Flower & Hayes, 1981) "compete for limited resources within working memory" (McCutchen, 2006, p. 122). Thus, supporting a historical essay's argument with evidence appears to be difficult for students, not only because they don't think about history in terms of interpretation and evidence, but also because of the complexity of the writing process itself.

PRACTICES THAT HELP STUDENTS WRITE HISTORICAL ARGUMENTS

Research in history education gives us some clues about how to encourage the transformation of knowledge in writing and discourage knowledge telling or regurgitation of information. In particular, the following practices support students' argument writing:

- Present history as an inquiry-oriented subject and engage students in investigating central questions that have multiple plausible interpretations.
- Structure reading opportunities, supporting both general reading comprehension and historical reading practices.
- Examine and discuss multiple historical sources that reflect multiple perspectives.
- Provide explicit instruction in the expectations for historical writing.
- Consider examples of good historical writing.
- Offer prewriting opportunities that emphasize analysis and interpretation.

The nature of tasks and instruction also influence the development of students' argument writing in history classrooms. Case studies of real-world classrooms lend further insight into teaching students to write historically despite certain dispositions. Young and Leinhardt (1998) found that AP U.S.

history students moved from listing information to synthesizing historical texts into an argument in response to a series of AP document-based essay questions. The initial phase of development revealed that the students were making the evidence fit a claim rather than developing a claim as they interpreted the evidence. Greene (1994) found that problem-based writing tasks encouraged college students to integrate their ideas and information from sources into arguments more than writing reports did. Within Australian schools, Coffin (2006) found that students at higher grade levels tend toward argument writing whereas students at lower grade levels tend toward reports, and these findings are consistent with the assignments given to children at these levels. Within high school, Monte-Sano and De La Paz (2012) found that writing tasks asking students to pretend they were a person in the past resulted in weaker historical thinking than do those that focus on authors of primary sources or analysis of the texts themselves.

Researcher interventions have also contributed to our understanding of teaching writing in history. Voss and Wiley (2000) found that students who used multiple texts and wrote an argumentative essay emerged with a deeper understanding of the content than any other combination of text use and writing task. De La Paz (2005) found that middle school students exposed to instruction in thinking historically and making arguments in writing produced more accurate and persuasive essays regardless of their incoming skills. In her study, she explicitly taught students particular ways of thinking historically and what writing an argument in history involves. Her work, along with Greene's, clarifies that writers' sense of the goals and structure of what they are writing are important influences on their final product. Further, Felton and Herko (2004) found that scaffolding—in the form of structured reading activities, oral debate, and reflection—improved high school students' abilities to write persuasive essays.

In our own research, we followed two expert high school history teachers whose students have improved on measures of evidence-based argument writing over time (Monte-Sano, 2012a). In these classrooms focused on historical thinking and writing (using the practices outlined in the bullets above), students demonstrated disciplinary thinking and use of evidence in their essays by the end of each course. We found five historical qualities present in these adolescents' writing (Monte-Sano, 2012b), including factual and interpretive accuracy, persuasiveness of evidence, sourcing of evidence, corroboration of evidence, and contextualization of evidence. In a collaborative project, Monte-Sano, De La Paz, and Felton (2014) found that struggling and advanced eighth-graders' historical thinking and argument writing improved with explicit instruction in historical reading and writing alongside opportunities to investigate historical questions using adapted primary sources and supporting disciplinary literacy tools.

CONCLUDING THOUGHTS

Research on reading and writing in history demonstrates that although students may not enter classrooms with advanced literacy and disciplinary thinking skills, carefully crafted classroom environments, tasks, and curriculum materials can have a positive influence on their learning. Teachers can make a difference.

Historians and literacy experts alike want to see adolescents move toward analytical thinking, reading, and writing. The International Reading Association (IRA) recommends that adolescents learn strategies such as "questioning themselves about what they read . . . recognizing how a text is organized . . . judging their own understanding . . . and evaluating authors' ideas and perspectives" (Moore, Bean, Birdyshaw, & Rycik, 1999, p. 5). The *Writing Next* report (Graham & Perin, 2007) calls on teachers to use writing as a means of learning in all content areas in order to support the development of adolescents' literacy practices. And literacy and history education researchers have learned a great deal about how students learn these practices and ways of thinking.

As Moje and her colleagues (2004) argue, an integral part of learning a discipline involves learning the oral and written language of the discipline. We would add to this charge that historians and history educators emphasize the role of advanced literacy in the teaching of history. This need for disciplinary orientation not only means providing a focus on reading and writing, but also involves explicitly framing courses around disciplinary concepts and ways of thinking. As teachers of history—whether in teacher education or history courses—our charge is to integrate the teaching of reading and writing into courses that highlight the interpretive nature of history and the higher-order thinking necessary to historical study. We share examples from our experiences in hopes of supporting teachers who want to integrate disciplinary reading and writing into their history classrooms.

SCENARIOS

SCENARIO 1: When Reading Is a Struggle

The setting: Molly Ferguson teaches the required eighth-grade U.S. history course in a large, suburban middle school. European Americans make up 68 percent of the student population, with 13 percent Latino/a and 13 percent African American students. Fifty-four percent of the student population qualifies for free or reduced-price meals.

The characters: Molly has an undergraduate degree in social studies education and is currently enrolled in nighttime master's degree courses.

The context: Molly's coursework focuses on integrating primary sources into the social studies classroom. During her coursework, Molly's professors often encourage her to create lessons using the Library of Congress's online resources, along with the resources provided through the National Archives.

Many of Molly's students have only ever been asked to work with the one resource the teacher is usually given—the textbook. In most of the history classes at Molly's school, if the students need reading remediation, the teachers share information by lecturing to students and having them copy information from the textbook. All the while, the students become increasingly bored with the subject. Most of Molly's colleagues have never taken advantage of the potential opportunity to teach students how to read for both comprehension and historical understanding.

The dilemma: Many of Molly's students struggle with reading comprehension and are enrolled in basic reading courses. In addition, many students are enrolled in intervention courses during lunch that are aimed at preparing the students to pass the state-mandated assessments. In past history courses, students have simply listened to teachers for information or used the textbook. Molly is perplexed by the challenge of trying to bring in lessons she creates using rich primary sources when basic reading comprehension is a struggle for her kids.

The "solution": Molly is very frustrated by the existing system that involves lecturing and having students copy passages from the textbook, and she finds that her students are in great need of remediation. To begin, Molly outlines her curriculum and recognizes her content priorities: what historical concepts students need to understand versus what information they merely need to be familiar with (see Wiggins & McTighe, 2005, p. 71). For example, students need to understand the "big idea" of judicial review. It is important for students to know certain court cases like *Marbury v. Madison*, while other cases or key details about cases might simply warrant familiarity. From there, she identifies background information and a range of primary sources to be used to highlight these priorities in a deeper, more meaningful way from what is currently being provided in the short textbook material. Molly then plans teaching units that will allow her students to use the textbook for background information and read primary sources to investigate these topics in greater depth.

To begin her class on this journey, Molly decides students will keep weekly "reading logs" of textbook information. The logs allow her to keep track of county-mandated content learning. Next, she creates primary source lessons that encourage students to engage in "in-depth" investigations and add their own contributions to the textbook. Before giving primary sources to students, she modifies and adapts documents to align with and stretch her students' reading levels (e.g., Wineburg & Martin, 2009). For guidance, she visits the website Historical Thinking Matters for examples of documents that have been adapted for struggling readers.[5] When possible, she uses existing materials rather than creating her own.

In adapting documents, Molly first identifies words that may be too challenging for her students unless she provides additional support. She then creates vocabulary banks to help her readers decode these words. In some cases, Molly replaces words when the vocabulary seems too advanced and the adaptation does not interfere greatly with the historical context. Molly also sets the goal of using sources that are less than one page long. She further includes background information that encourages students to read for basic comprehension—the literal reading of the text such that they follow the unfolding of the historical account—first. Students read the documents and use a simple note-taking guide to help them think critically about the material. She asks students to answer questions such as the following:

- Who is the source of the document? What do we know about the author's perspective?
- What in this document relates to the textbook reading? What is different from and similar to the textbook and other readings?
- When and where was this document created? What else was going on at the time that might have influenced its creation?
- What new learning did you gain from this document? How does this document extend, support, or challenge what you understood already?

To wrap up their thinking, students write paragraphs analyzing the sources they have used in class or build an argument based on those sources.

The rationale for the instruction: Molly's practices showcase the benefits of using primary sources to empower students to become better readers. By scaffolding the reading experience for learners, Molly helps her students comprehend texts and think historically. Writing arguments helps students process their reading more effectively than would simply writing summaries.

Questions for Reflection

1. Think through your own efforts to teach literacy in your social studies or history classes. What has worked well? What has not worked well? What do you think would have helped you do better or what have been the major challenges you've faced?

2. In what ways is Molly teaching historical literacy?

3. How does outlining her curriculum help guide Molly's teaching practices? In what ways does this strengthen and limit Molly's teaching of content?

4. In what ways do "in-depth" historical investigations help promote historical literacy in the classroom? What are the challenges associated with these investigations? How does Molly attempt to overcome these challenges?

5. What resources does Molly consult to help her achieve her pedagogical goals? What resources have been helpful to you as you've tried to integrate history and literacy?

SCENARIO 2: Shifting the Focus in History Class to Embrace the Common Core

The setting: Charles Tam teaches at a large, urban public high school. The largest demographic of students at Charles's school is African American (43 percent), followed by Latino/a (36 percent), and smaller groups of European American and Asian American students (10 or 11 percent each). Forty-two percent of these students qualify for the free and reduced-price meals program. Eighty-two percent of students graduate from Charles's school.

The characters: Charles, a ten-year veteran, teaches a ninth-grade World History course. He earned his bachelor's degree in social studies education and is currently working on his master's degree in secondary teaching.

The context: This school year, Charles's district supervisor has asked that all social studies teachers focus on bringing certain areas of the Common Core State Standards into the classroom, specifically reading, writing, and speaking. The supervisor has encouraged each teacher to use primary sources to help students gain a deeper appreciation for what those literacy skills look like in a history classroom.

The dilemma: Charles has been teaching the content of the course for several years. He has detailed lecture notes and presentations that address the specifics of the course. Now, he believes he needs to shift his focus from learning content to learning *skills and content.* Specifically, students need to be able to read, write, speak, and listen in the history classroom. He recognizes that in the past, his focus on only content led students to see history as a fixed set of facts. He knows that if he is to emphasize the skills of historical thinking, students will need to understand that history is interpretive—that based on evidence, they can draw their own conclusions that might differ from their peers' or those of authorities. Charles realizes that to help students shift their mental approach, he will need to expand their understanding of history and build their capacity to read and write historically, something most ninth-grade students have never been asked to do.

The "solution": On the first day of class, Charles decides to assess his students' incoming thinking and skills. He gives his students a political cartoon from World War II, along with a diary entry from a survivor of the Holocaust. He asks them to tell him everything they can figure out about the source and context of the documents. As he reads student responses, he notices that most of his students will need a lot of guidance in how to read historically. Many students leave the question blank, attempt to answer the question without using details from the documents, or summarize the information in the documents.

Charles decides he will have to help his students see that history is open to interpretation. He selects a lesson format called an "Opening Up the Textbook" or an OUT (Martin & Monte-Sano, 2007). This activity helps students take a topic addressed in the textbook and examine it closely using primary source materials. Charles uses an OUT to guide his students in a thorough evaluation of the explorer Christopher Columbus. Using Fordham University's digital Modern History Sourcebook archive, Charles pulls primary sources from Christopher Columbus's journals.[6] He asks his students to read the different journals and decide whether they think Columbus should be remembered as "a star or a scoundrel." As students read each document, they record details and form a conclusion about Columbus. As an assessment, students rewrite the textbook section about Columbus, showcasing their answer to the original OUT question. Students begin to see that they have a voice in history.

Charles also decides he needs to give his students more structure in learning to read historical documents. He finds that the primary source analysis sheet from the Library of Congress serves as a helpful teaching tool to prompt his students' thinking about documents. Throughout the school year, he encourages students to use this sheet when looking at any primary source. He gives students a copy of the analysis sheet on cardstock and frequently urges them to use the three steps—observe, reflect, and question—when examining any document. For the first semester, Charles thinks aloud as he models how to read sources as historians do by emphasizing the source and context of each document as well as by comparing documents. Before each lesson, he writes down exactly what he "thinks" as he looks at each primary source. Then, he picks out a few observations of the document that he can read out loud to students. He reads and annotates the document aloud so students can see his approach firsthand. During class, he underlines the source and discusses the point of view of the author. He keeps track of his observations on the document or in the "observe" column of the analysis sheet. He also includes guided practice by asking questions to prompt students' thinking. Students gradually begin annotating the documents and questioning the different texts.

The rationale for the instruction: As the second marking period draws to a close, Charles finds that, without prompting, his students begin to annotate the documents as they complete the "observe" step of the process. Halfway through the school year, Charles assigns his first writing essay that asks students to use documents to find a common theme in world history. As the year goes on, Charles is delighted to find that his young ninth graders have significantly improved their historical reading. His students look for the source and contexts of different documents. They question the authors and identify multiple perspectives on a topic. He sees that a focus on what he had previously thought of as "skills" has actually helped his students know history—that skills and content play an integrated role in studying history.

Questions for Reflection

1. In what ways are history teachers like Charles struggling with teaching both content and subject area practices (such as reading, writing, and thinking skills)?

2. To what extent do you feel that history teachers should be concerned with the Common Core? As teachers try to address the Common Core's emphasis on literacy practices and content, what support do they need? What helps Charles transform his teaching?

3. How does Charles use a think-aloud approach (or modeling) to help scaffold his students' learning of historical reading? What role, if any, do you see for thinking aloud in order to model historical practices in your own teaching?

4. What historical practices does Charles help students develop in his classroom? What practices do students need to develop more in his classroom? What historical practices do you see students struggle with in your classroom? What practices do you struggle to teach?

5. How does Charles assess his students' historical practices? How have you tried to assess students' historical practices in your classroom? How might assessments of historical practices differ from conventional assessments of historical content?

SCENARIO 3: Transitioning From Writing Summary to Argument

The setting: Kate Bobeck teaches the required eleventh-grade humanities course in a small public charter school in a large urban area. The student population is almost evenly split among European American, African American, Latino/a, and Asian American students. Twenty-five percent of students have been identified as learning disabled. Thirty-two percent of students are enrolled in the free and reduced-price meals program. The vast majority speak English as a first language.

The characters: Kate has a bachelor's degree in history and a master's degree in teaching history. She has been teaching for ten years and is committed to developing her students' evidence-based writing.

The context: At the beginning of each school year, Kate finds that her students are not yet proficient in writing arguments. When students are asked to answer a historical question, they may address the question in their opening sentence, or closing paragraph, without remaining focused on it. Students also may not present a claim, provide support for their claim, explain how their support serves as evidence through the inclusion of a warrant, address counter-claims, or close with historical insight.

The dilemma: Kate requires her students to write essays every two weeks. She realizes that students will not write arguments automatically and that she needs to make time to teach them to write evidence-based arguments in history, in light of students' incoming skills.

The "solution": Kate recognizes that one reason students tend to write summaries for history essays is that history is typically framed as a set of given information, and history classes tend to focus on the transmission of facts. Such instruction inhibits students' historical reasoning and ability to see the potential for argument in history. Kate knows that one major step toward writing arguments in history will involve shifting students' conception of what history entails so they can develop a more evidence-based interpretation. Consequently, her first step in helping students shift from summary to argument is to frame history as evidence-based interpretation throughout the school year. She accomplishes this goal by

- focusing units of study on a central inquiry question,
- selecting a range of primary and secondary documents to investigate this question,
- giving students opportunities to construct their own interpretations of the inquiry question both in discussion and in writing, and
- helping them to anticipate and rebut counterarguments by having them critique one another's essay drafts.

In terms of writing, Kate offers a combination of explicit instruction in text structure and claim development and guided practice in constructing outlines and theses. Kate explicitly teaches her students how to write an argument by directly modeling different aspects of an essay and guiding students in their practice of such skills. For example, Kate explains what a claim is, models it, and asks her students to evaluate and improve a sample claim in class where they can debrief and ask questions (see Appendix A; for further reading on teaching argumentative writing, see Hillocks, 2011; Smagorinsky, Johannessen, Kahn, & McCann, 2011; and Smith, Wilhelm, & Fredricksen, 2012). Then her students write their own claim for homework and share it with her for feedback the following day. She models and guides similarly how to write an outline and an introductory paragraph. Each unit of study ends with an essay and includes modeling and practice in different aspects of writing.

The rationale for the instruction: Kate's practice involves a combination of explicit instruction and a constructivist approach in which students have opportunities to inquire about historical topics and develop interpretations of the past. She finds that this approach works especially well to serve those students with weak incoming skills.

Questions for Reflection

1. Think about all of the times students put pen to paper (or fingers to keyboard) in your classroom to write. What kinds of writing do you ask your students to do already (including anything from notes to short answers to research papers)? Share examples.

2. To what extent do the types of writing emphasized by the Common Core differ from the kinds of writing your students typically do in your classes? What support do you or other teachers need to integrate Common Core writing standards into your classes?

3. Does adhering to the Common Core standards change your teaching for the better? What do you see as worthwhile and counterproductive in meeting these standards in your teaching?

4. In what ways does Kate's use of the inquiry method help students learn to read, think, and write historically? How does this method help foster an academically focused classroom?

5. What challenges do different students face during historical inquires? In what ways can teachers differentiate instruction to meet the needs of all students?

6. In what ways does Kate provide support for her students during historical investigations? What additional supports might she use to help her students?

SCENARIO 4: Helping Students Use and Select "Good" Evidence

The setting: Vince Lyle works in a small independent school in a large urban area. Of the 295 students enrolled at the school, 27 percent are students of color. In the class of seventeen, five students are African American, one is Asian American, and all students speak English as their first language. One marker of socioeconomic status (SES) indicates that 24 percent of the student body receives financial aid.

The characters: Vince has taught history for twenty-five years. In this class, he teaches the required eleventh-grade U.S. history course.

The context: In his classroom, Vince, who has an advanced degree in history, talks about and models teaching history as an inquiry-based subject. Vince is committed to developing his students' writing and historical thinking. Vince creates clear classroom routines and encourages daily writing and discussion. His students' interpretations of texts are welcomed and encouraged, especially when grounded in specific passages of the texts. He gives students opportunities to write analyses of historical sources multiple times per week. Additional writing opportunities serve as summative assessments of entire units of study and build on prior classroom discussions.

The dilemma: Vince finds that when he pushes students to incorporate examples to support their written arguments, they may include a quotation or an example that is not relevant to their argument. Alternately, students focus on their personal opinions or examples from their lives today rather than integrating examples from the historical topic to bolster their arguments. Vince knows that if students are to write compelling, coherent, historical arguments, they need to learn to ground their arguments in evidence and be more judicious in their choice of that evidence. He would like to take steps to help students ground their written arguments in evidence, and to ensure that they select and incorporate "good" evidence versus seemingly random examples.

The "solution": Vince's general approach to teaching history frames his solution to this dilemma. Vince centers each unit on a central question and selects relevant texts to facilitate students' investigation of the question. He teaches history as evidence-based interpretation: History is not a list of facts to be memorized, but a series of questions to investigate. Students in his classes regularly read historical texts, including primary documents and excerpts of historians' monographs. Vince frames texts as interpretations to be questioned and puzzled over, not read as the authoritative final say (as is often the case in classrooms that primarily rely on textbooks). Vince puts students in the role of developing their own interpretations, supporting those interpretations with examples, and using argumentative warrants to explain how the examples serve as evidence for their interpretive claims. Students are required to play an active role in figuring out their own arguments, rather than only listening to the arguments of others.

To help students incorporate evidence effectively in their essays, Vince uses two strategies to improve students' reading and analysis of historical texts that can be referred to as evidence in their arguments: annotations and mini-writes. For each reading, Vince directs students to annotate the text by making marginal notes that include questions, connections to other texts or events, and interpretations (see Figure 2A.1 in Appendix B). In annotating, students underline words or write notes, questions, and ideas in the margins. Vince's practice of annotating directly links reading and writing for improved comprehension. Students interact with and begin the process of interpreting texts. Vince helps his students learn to annotate by giving specific directions, analyzing text together in class, and giving feedback on their annotations. When he asks students to annotate their readings, he pushes them to become active readers engaged with the texts in many ways:

- asking and answering questions of themselves and the author,
- monitoring comprehension,
- making connections to prior knowledge and other texts,
- integrating reading and writing, and
- summarizing.

In Vince's classroom, the interaction with texts emphasizes the source and context of documents. The particularities of where he directs students' attention are historical in nature and support the students' comprehension, inference, and interpretation skills. For example, Vince asks students to draw a big "S" over the phrases in the Constitution that protect Southern interests. Such a directive gives students a purpose for reading the document, and it connects their reading to a larger inquiry on the causes of the Civil War. When one student continues to struggle with incorporating examples, Vince looks at the student's notebook and discovers that the student hasn't been annotating documents. Vince is able to follow up and give this student further support in learning to annotate documents. The notebooks also provide evidence of the students' growth throughout the year. One student begins the year with more literal comments that are focused on comprehension of text and then transitions to writing interpretive comments and interacting with the text.

Reading and analysis regularly lead to writing in these classes; reading and writing are intertwined. But Vince's teaching does not emphasize standard aspects of essay writing such as how to form a claim or construct an outline. Instead, he integrates writing as a means of learning to think historically by asking students to analyze documents they have annotated in regular informal writing prompts (mini-writes). Mini-writes give students an opportunity to read documents carefully, comprehend them, and situate them historically (see Appendix C for samples of such prompts). Typically, students complete these informal essays at the beginning of class, and the writing is analytical in nature, emphasizing close reading of the text. This analytic focus gives students the chance to make sense of a single author's perspective or issue and to interact with the text. These assignments ask students to begin a consideration of the past with an exploration of the evidence rather than depicting their own personal views.

Once students compose several mini-writes on the different perspectives and discuss the sources in class, Vince then assigns a second kind of prompt: an interpretive synthesis of complex topics using a wider range of sources. This writing is done at home, allowing students to pull together ideas regarding a topic they have been considering for an extended period of time. In order to complete them, students have to corroborate various documents related to one topic, read and see the documents together, and synthesize perspectives about which they have already written.

The rationale for the instruction: The setup detailed above, an interpretive synthesis assignment given after several micro-level writing assignments on the same topic, scaffolds student writing. As students synthesize across sources to write argumentative essays, they can fall back on their solid understanding of sources and their informal essays about the reliability and meaning of individual sources. In Vince's classroom, teaching historical thinking advances students' historical writing.

Questions for Reflection

1. In what ways does Vince promote a classroom environment focused on historical investigations?

2. Do you find that your students include good evidence to support their reasoning? If so, what do you think has helped them do so? If not, what do you think are the obstacles that stand in their way?

3. In order to address his goal of helping students write responses grounded in evidence, Vince uses annotations and mini-writes. How does each strategy help support his goals? What challenges does each strategy pose for teachers and students?

4. How does forming central unit questions help promote historical literacy? What are the benefits of using central questions in the classroom?

5. How does Vince assess his students' historical reading and writing?

SCENARIO 5: Balancing the Coverage Mandate With Historical Inquiry

The setting: Tasha Guyer teaches the required tenth-grade U.S. history course in her traditional comprehensive high school. Her students come from a mix of suburban and rural communities. Families of students at her school are mostly characterized as middle class. The student population is about half European American and 25 percent each from African American and Latino/a families. Her school is very focused on increasing the number of students who pass the state's high-stakes assessments, and administrators put pressure on teachers to cover as much content as possible.

The characters: Tasha received her bachelor's degree in history and earned her master's degree in social studies education. Her master's coursework included instruction in historical reading and writing. During her program, she created multiple units based around essential questions and thinking-based learning.

The context: On her first day of teaching, Tasha walks in with grand ideas of filling her new history class with in-depth, multiday primary source lessons and projects. Her goal is to teach deep historical thinking by implementing student-centered, project-based learning activities. However, when she arrives, she is handed her curriculum, textbook, and district-created unit tests. Her tenth-grade U.S. history curriculum is broken down into seven units.

The dilemma: As she looks over the curriculum, Tasha finds that with her 180 days of teaching, the idea of using multiple projects will need to be revised. She learns that any in-class analysis will have to be limited to one- or two-day lessons. She wonders how she can fit curriculum goals, district assessments, and in-depth primary source lessons into that short forty-five-minute period.

The "solution": Tasha first looks closely at the curriculum guide and identifies two or three topics per unit that can be easily investigated using primary sources. She decides to mix content-specific learning with primary source-based activities. She uses different means of helping students learn background information including video clips, mini lectures, and reading but spends most of her classroom time leading the students in historical investigations. She then uses document-based inquiry, structured debates, and one-day activities that ask students to evaluate the source and context of documents in order to fulfill her goal of using primary-source activities. For example, the curriculum devotes a lot of attention to African American rights after the Civil War. She begins with an inquiry question, "Were African Americans free after the Civil War?" which leads into productive discussions of several related curriculum topics. Many of these topics are covered in the assessment and can be easily supplemented by a series of primary source documents. Tasha creates her lesson using the National History Education Clearinghouse's "Structured Academic Controversy" teaching guide.[7] Each primary source document includes an introduction with historical background, while the documents allow students the opportunity for historical investigation. As an assessment, students answer the inquiry question in an essay format, using the documents.

Similarly, Tasha creates a lesson surrounding the content of the rise of big business and progressive reform. She creates a structured debate around the question "Were the industrialist leaders heroes or villains?" She uses the National Archive's "Docs Teach" site[8] to accumulate documents from the time period. Using their template, she creates her own "weighing the evidence" activity and has students work in teams in the computer lab. Students examine an array of documents and place them on a scale from "hero" to "villain." As an assessment, the students defend their responses in an in-class debate.

The rationale for the instruction: The example lessons discussed above take three or four classroom days. However, the lessons contain information spanning multiple dimensions of the curriculum, allowing Tasha to teach historical thinking skills while keeping pace with the district mandates. Creating and adding to a timeline of related events helps students keep track of specific events in each era.

By allowing students the opportunity to deeply explore district-mandated curriculum through primary source evaluation, Tasha fosters a classroom environment driven by student thinking. The students enjoy the thorough investigations and remember the content better because it now has meaning and purpose.

Questions for Reflection

1. How are Tasha's pedagogical goals limited and supported by her local school system? What other barriers do teachers face? What constraints and supports do you see in your school system for inquiry-based teaching of history and social studies?

2. What do you think are the most compelling reasons to balance inquiry and content coverage? What do you think are the greatest challenges to balancing inquiry with coverage? What might help you integrate inquiry and content coverage within your courses?

3. In what ways does Tasha adapt her plans to balance teaching historical practices and the required content? How does Tasha's approach move along the teaching continuum—from more teacher-directed lessons to student-centered lessons?

4. How do the Common Core State Standards support inquiry-based teaching? What barriers do teachers face when focusing on an inquiry-based method?

5. How are students learning to be historical thinkers in Tasha's classroom?

REFERENCES

Afflerbach, P., & VanSledright, B. (2001). Hath! Doth! What? Middle graders reading innovative history text. *Journal of Adolescent & Adult Literacy, 44*(8), 696–707.

Ashby, R., Lee, P., & Shemilt, D. (2005). Putting principles into practice: Teaching and planning. In M. S. Donovan & J. D. Bransford (Eds.), *How students learn: History in the classroom* (pp. 79–178). Washington, DC: National Academies Press.

Bain, R. (2005). They thought the world was flat: Applying the principles of how people learn in teaching high school history. In M. S. Donovan & J. D. Bransford (Eds.), *How students learn: History in the classroom* (pp. 179–214). Washington, DC: National Academies Press.

Bain, R. (2006). Rounding up unusual suspects: Facing the authority hidden in the history classroom. *Teachers College Record, 108,* 2080–2114.

Bazerman, C., & Paradis, J. G. (Eds.). (1991). *Textual dynamics of the professions: Historical and contemporary studies of writing in professional communities.* Madison, WI: University of Wisconsin Press. Retrieved April 1, 2014, from http://wac.colostate.edu/books/textual_dynamics/

Bereiter, C., & Scardamalia, M. (1987). *The psychology of written composition.* Hillsdale, NJ: Erlbaum.

Braten, I., & Stromso, H. (2006). Constructing meaning from multiple information sources as a function of personal epistemology. *Information Design Journal, 14*(1), 56–67.

Britt, M. A., & Aglinskas, C. (2002). Improving students' ability to identify and use source information. *Cognition and Instruction, 20*(4), 485–522.

Coffin, C. (2006). *Historical discourse: The language of time, cause, and evaluation.* London, UK: Continuum.

Collingwood, R. G. (1993). *The idea of history.* Oxford, UK: Clarendon Press.

Collins, A., Brown, J. S., & Holum, A. (1991). Cognitive apprenticeship: Making thinking visible. *American Educator, 15*(3), 6–11.

Council of Chief State School Officers (CCSSO). (2010). *Common Core State Standards for English language arts and literacy in history/social studies, science, and technical subjects.* Washington, DC: National Governors Association Center for Best Practices, CCSSO. Retrieved August 27, 2012, from http://www.core standards.org/ELA-Literacy/

De La Paz, S. (2005). Effects of historical reasoning instruction and writing strategy mastery in culturally and academically diverse middle school classrooms. *Journal of Educational Psychology, 97*(2), 139–156.

Edwards, A. D. (1978). The "language of history" and the communication of historical knowledge. In A. K. Dickinson & P. J. Lee (Eds.), *History teaching and historical understanding* (pp. 54–71). London, UK: Heinemann.

Felton, M., & Herko, S. (2004). From dialogue to two-sided argument: Scaffolding adolescents' persuasive writing. *Journal of Adolescent & Adult Literacy, 47*(8), 672–683.

Flower, L., & Hayes, J. (1981). A cognitive process theory of writing. *College Composition and Communication, 32*(4), 365–387.

Flower, L., Stein, V., Ackerman, J., Kantz, P., McCormick, K., & Peck, W. (1990). *Reading to write: Exploring a cognitive and social process.* New York, NY: Oxford University Press.

Graham, S., & Perin, D. (2007). *Writing next: Effective strategies to improve writing of adolescents in middle and high schools—A report to Carnegie Corporation of New York.* Washington, DC: Alliance for Excellent Education. Retrieved April 2009 from http://www.a114ed.org/files/WritingNext.pdf

Greene, S. (1994). The problems of learning to think like a historian: Writing history in the culture of the classroom. *Educational Psychologist, 29*(2), 89–96.

Greene, S., & Ackerman, J. (1996). Expanding the constructivist metaphor: A rhetorical perspective on literacy research and practice. *Review of Educational Research, 65*(4), 383–420.

Hexter, J. H. (1971). *The history primer.* New York, NY: Basic Books.

Hillocks, G. (2011). *Teaching argument writing, Grades 6–12: Supporting claims with relevant evidence and clear reasoning.* Portsmouth, NH: Heinemann.

Hynd, C. (1999). Teaching students to think critically using multiple texts in history. *Journal of Adolescent and Adult Literacy, 42*(6), 428–436.

Hynd-Shanahan, C., Holschuh, J. P., & Hubbard, B. P. (2004). Thinking like a historian: College students' reading of multiple historical documents. *Journal of Literacy Research, 36*(2), 141–176.

Martin, D., & Monte-Sano, C. (2007). Inquiry, controversy, and ambiguous texts: Learning to teach for historical thinking. In W. Warren & D. Cantu (Eds.), *History education 101: The past, present, and future of teacher preparation* (pp. 167–186). Charlotte, NC: Information Age Publishing.

McCutchen, D. (2006). Cognitive factors in the development of children's writing. In C. MacArthur, S. Graham, & J. Fitzgerald (Eds.), *Handbook of writing research* (pp. 115–130). New York, NY: Guilford.

Mink, L. (1987). *Historical understanding.* Ithaca, NY: Cornell University Press.

Moje, E., Ciechanowski, K., Kramer, K., Ellis, L., Carrillo, R., & Collazo, T. (2004). Working toward third space in content area literacy: An examination of everyday funds of knowledge and discourse. *Reading Research Quarterly, 39*(1), 38–70.

Monte-Sano, C. (2012a). Build skills by doing history. *Phi Delta Kappan, 94*(3), 62–65.

Monte-Sano, C. (2012b). What makes a good history essay? Assessing historical aspects of argumentative writing. *Social Education, 76*(6), 294–298.

Monte-Sano, C., & De La Paz, S. (2012). Using writing tasks to elicit adolescents' historical reasoning. *Journal of Literacy Research, 44*(3), 273–299.

Monte-Sano, C., De La Paz, S., & Felton, M. (2014). *Reading, thinking, and writing about history: Teaching argument writing to diverse learners in the Common Core classroom, Grades 6–12.* New York, NY: Teachers College Press.

Moore, D., Bean, T., Birdyshaw, D., & Rycik, J. (1999). *Adolescent literacy: A position statement for the Commission on Adolescent Literacy of the International Reading Association.* Retrieved July 2007 from http://www.reading.org/downloads/positions/ps1036_adolescent.pdf

National Center for Education Statistics. (2007). *The nation's report card: Reading 2007.* Retrieved February 20, 2010, from http://nces.ed.gov/pubsearch/pubsinfo.asp?pubid=2007496

National Center for Education Statistics. (2008). *The nation's report card: Writing 2007.* Retrieved February 10, 2010, from http://nces.ed.gov/pubsearch/pubsinfo.asp?pubid=2008468

National Council for the Social Studies. (2013). *The college, career, and civic life (C3) framework for social studies state standards.* Silver Spring, MD: Author.

Nokes, J. D., Dole, J. A., & Hacker, D. J. (2007). Teaching high school students to use heuristics while reading historical texts. *Journal of Educational Psychology, 99*(3), 492–504.

Paxton, R. (2002). The influence of author visibility on high school students solving a historical problem. *Cognition and Instruction, 20,* 197–248.

Perfetti, C., Britt, M. A., & Georgi, M. C. (1995). *Text-based learning and reasoning: Studies in history.* Mahwah, NJ: Erlbaum.

Reisman, A. (2012). The "document-based lesson": Bringing disciplinary inquiry into high school history classrooms with adolescent struggling readers. *Journal of Curriculum Studies, 44,* 233–264.

Rouet, J. F., Britt, M. A., Mason, R., & Perfetti, C. A. (1996). Using multiple sources of evidence to reason about history. *Journal of Educational Psychology, 88*(3), 478–493.

Rouet, J. F., Favart, M., Britt, M. A., & Perfetti, C. A. (1997). Studying and using multiple documents in history: Effects of discipline expertise. *Cognition and Instruction, 15*(1), 85–106.

Smagorinsky, P., Johannessen, L. R., Kahn, E. A., & McCann, T. M. (2011). *Teaching students to write argument.* Portsmouth, NH: Heinemann.

Smith, M. W., Wilhelm, J. D., & Fredricksen, J. E. (2012). *Oh, yeah?! Putting argument to work both in school and out.* Portsmouth, NH: Heinemann.

Stahl, S., Hynd, C., Britton, B., McNish, M., & Bosquet, D. (1996). What happens when students read multiple source documents in history? *Reading Research Quarterly, 31*(4), 430–456.

Toulmin, S. (1958). *The uses of argument.* New York, NY: Cambridge University Press.

Voss, J., & Wiley, J. (2000). A case study of developing historical understanding via instruction: The importance of integrating text components and constructing arguments. In P. Stearns, P. Seixas, & S. Wineburg (Eds.), *Knowing, teaching, and learning history: National and international perspectives* (pp. 375–389). New York, NY: New York University Press.

Wiggins, G., & McTighe, J. (2005). *Understanding by design* (2nd ed.). Alexandria, VA: ASCD.

Wiley, J., & Voss, J. F. (1999). Constructing arguments from multiple sources: Tasks that promote understanding and not just memory for text. *Journal of Educational Psychology, 91*(2), 301–311.

Wineburg, S. (2001). *Historical thinking and other unnatural acts: Charting the future of teaching the past.* Philadelphia, PA: Temple University Press.

Wineburg, S., & Martin, D. (2009). Tampering with history: Adapting primary sources for struggling readers. *Social Education, 73*(5), 212–216.

Wolfe, M., & Goldman, S. (2005). Relations between adolescents' text processing and reasoning. *Cognition and Instruction, 23*(4), 467–502.

Young, K. M., & Leinhardt, G. (1998). Writing from primary documents: A way of knowing in history. *Written Communication, 15*(1), 25–68.

NOTES

1. Historical Thinking Matters is a collaboration between the Stanford History Education Group, Stanford University, and the Center for History and New Media, George Mason University. The documents and the task to compare them came from the Historical Thinking Matters website: http://historical thinkingmatters.org/spanishamericanwar/0/inquiry/intro/.

2. For the full excerpt of the student's think aloud and an analysis of it, go to http://historicalthinkingmatters.org/spanishamericanwar/1/studentwork/ta1/.

3. See the Reading Like a Historian curriculum resources at http://sheg.stanford.edu/rlh for examples of these posters and introductory materials as well as the lessons.

4. The latter is a practice advocated by Wineburg and Martin (2009) in their article "Tampering With History."

5. See the Historical Thinking Matters curriculum at www.historicalthinkingmatters.org for the full site. Each primary source has a set of historical reading questions, and sources have been adapted for struggling readers. For a guide to adapting sources, go to the "Teachers" section of any of the curriculum modules and find worksheets under "Materials."

6. You can find the Modern History Sourcebook at www.fordham.edu/Halsall/mod/modsbook.asp.

7. See http://teachinghistory.org/teaching-materials/teaching-guides/21731.

8. See http://docsteach.org.

Appendix A

Making the Writing Process Explicit by Modeling and Practicing Claim Writing

What makes a good claim? As we already know, a claim is our argument in the essay, the opinion that we are trying to prove. But what distinguishes a good one from a not-so-good one? Let's look at a few things . . .

See the grading rubric for our claim statements (below). Let's take a look at what these explanations mean. Read the examples below that respond to the question "What makes Frederick Douglass's autobiography an effective, persuasive narrative?"

APPROACHES STANDARDS

"Frederick Douglass wrote a persuasive piece because of his language, imagery, and content in the book."

What makes this statement "approach standards"? It

- answers the question accurately;
- addresses the various aspects of the argument (language, imagery, and content); and
- asserts an idea that can be reasonably proved in a five- to seven-paragraph essay

Now let's improve that claim.

MEETS STANDARDS

"Interesting content combined with clear language and strong metaphors make Frederick Douglass's autobiography a persuasive one."

What makes this statement "meets standards"? It

- addresses the first three points in the claim that approaches standards *and*

- provides more "thoughtful analysis" of the topic because of its assertions of "interesting content," "clear language," and "strong metaphors."

Now let's improve that claim even more.

EXCEEDS STANDARDS

"Repeated Christian imagery, vivid language, and an almost scientific attention to details make Frederick Douglass's autobiography a gripping abolitionist statement."
What makes this statement "exceed standards"?

- it addresses the first three points in the claim that approaches standards *and*
- there are more self-generated ideas in here. The author talks about "Christian imagery" and "vivid language" with a "scientific attention to details." These descriptors require more deep and complex analysis of the written work. Moreover, they show that the reader has come up with some interesting ideas of her or his own to discuss in the essay.

Now It's Your Turn

Write your claim or the claim of a classmate in the space below. Then rank it according to the rubric above and explain why you chose that evaluation. Finally, tweak or improve the claim to make it a bit more deep and complex. Sample claim:

Evaluation:

Exceeds standards   Meets standards   Approaches standards

Why did you choose that evaluation?

Now, improve the claim to make it more complex.

Appendix B

An Example of One Student's Annotations of a Primary Text in Vince's Class

Figure 2A.1

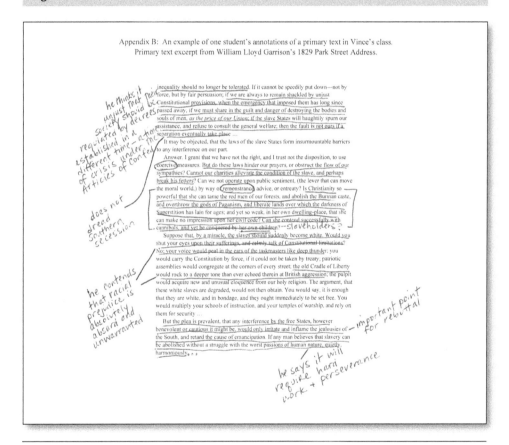

Appendix B: An example of one student's annotations of a primary text in Vince's class.
Primary text excerpt from William Lloyd Garrison's 1829 Park Street Address.

Source: Primary text excerpt from William Lloyd Garrison's 1829 Park Street Address.

Appendix C

Focusing Students' Attention on an Author's Purposes and Writing to Learn With Informal Mini-Writes

Mr. Lyle's Informal Writing Prompts

Frederick Douglass—5th of July. Closely, alertly, thoughtfully, and creatively survey the latest source, Frederick Douglass's 1852 speech in his adopted city of Rochester, New York. What is he aiming to do in this speech? How do you suppose he believed that this address would further and strengthen the abolitionist cause? What is he trying to tap into? Does he succeed—why? Why not—or hard to say? (Please explain) . . . (Writing prompt, October 18, 2004)

W.L. Garrison and Religion. Using the three Garrison documents from pp. 78–97 (1. The Park Street Address on July 4, 1829; 2. the Opening Editorial of the Liberator on January 1, 1831; and 3. the Declaration of Sentiments of the American Anti-Slavery Society in December 1833), please assess the place of religion in Garrison's thinking. What insights might your ideas provide in the study of the abolitionist movement?

Please do not begin to write immediately—survey the reading and your annotations; take a few notes and then begin. (Writing prompt, October 12, 2004)

3 Literacy in the Science Classroom

Kok-Sing Tang, Stephen C. Tighe, and Elizabeth Birr Moje

*L*iteracy is not a term often discussed among science educators. And yet, new standards in both science and English/Language Arts call for the teaching of literacy for scientific purposes within science classrooms. To many science teachers and students, however, the only time that literacy plays a role in science learning is when students are asked to read—a request that is usually limited to a textbook passage—or when they are expected to write laboratory reports. In this chapter, we illustrate through four cases drawn from science classrooms how science literacy development is not only a central dimension of learning science, but also, of necessity, the purview of the secondary science teacher. Our stance is that science teachers are the most appropriate educators to teach the literacy practices of science because they are the people with expertise in the content and practices of science. We also illustrate how students can deeply learn both science content and science literacy when they are fully engaged with the literacy practices of science.

Before turning to the cases, however, we provide some background on the concept of science literacy. Specifically, we show that science literacy is a part of the everyday practices of scientists and thus must be a dimension of science learning for students.

WHAT IS SCIENCE LITERACY, AND WHY DOES IT MATTER?

The term *science literacy* or *scientific literacy* is widely used in science education, particularly in influential official documents produced by the National Research Council (NRC), American Association for the Advancement of Science (AAAS), and Programme for International Student Assessment (PISA) of the Organisation for Economic Co-operation and Development (OECD). In these documents, however, scientific literacy is primarily about the development of a level of science knowledge necessary for laypeople to make informed decisions on science-related issues, such as choosing different health products or supporting certain environmental agendas. According to such notions of scientific literacy, people are usually considered to be literate in the sciences if they are knowledgeable about scientific facts, concepts, and processes, and if they understand their impact on society.

This understanding of scientific literacy (as a knowledge component) further exacerbates the lack of attention to the roles of reading, writing, and other literacy practices in the teaching and learning of science. The irony of this view—what Norris and Phillips (2002) refer to as the "derived" view of science literacy—is that the development of knowledge about science is largely dependent on understanding the *practices* of science, or the ways of doing, thinking, reading, writing, and talking science (Lemke, 1990). That is, science knowledge cannot be fully learned unless the learner is a participant in the literacy practices of science—the practices involved in using print, images, graphs, tables, and other symbolic systems to represent or access science information, ideas, or understandings.

This lack of focus on literacy in science education does not reflect the nature of scientific practices in real life. Anthropological studies of practicing scientists in laboratories and research centers have revealed the complex literacy tasks undertaken by scientists. For instance, Latour and Woolgar (1979) traced the written publications of scientists back to the material resources and semiotic actions undertaken in the research laboratory. They trace the process of scientific research from scientists' firsthand engagement with lab mice, chemical substance, apparatus, and machines, following it through to the abstract representation—the literacy process and products— of scribbled notes, codified labels, data tables, computer displays, graphs, written drafts, and ultimately to a polished academic paper accepted by the larger scientific community. Every stage of translation (e.g., from colored samples to a coded table, from scattered points to a continuous line graph) produced a series of inscriptions that selectively and systematically transformed some features of a material substance or previous data into parts of a larger set of evidences and arguments. Seen from Latour and Woolgar's perspective, scientific facts become established through a web of relationships among statements, which are themselves generated and backed by multiple chains of reading, writing, and investigation. In other words, scientific theory building involves a highly sophisticated literacy endeavor operating within a certain social and political structure. Scientific knowledge, rather than being objective, is thus constructed by scientists working within social conventions and practices.

At the same time, advances in the field of disciplinary literacy have given further support to the role of literacy in science teaching and learning. Literacy educators point out that the various knowledge components of scientific literacy would not be possible without the interpretation of texts, or *literacy* in Norris and Phillips's (2002) fundamental sense. Such views debunk the idea that students can comprehend a science text simply by decoding the words in it. Instead, the research acknowledges an intrinsic and reciprocal relationship between literacy (as textual interpretation, such as reading and writing) and scientific knowledge.

Furthermore, many who study literacy also argue that literacy skills are never autonomous (Street, 1984)—that is, independent of how they are used within communities of practice—and that more or less specialized domains of literate *practice* can use skills in differing ways. Some distinguish between these differences by referring to *generic* versus *disciplinary* skills (Shanahan & Shanahan, 2008). They argue that some skills are basic literacy skills, generic to all subject matters, and that people progress to specialized disciplinary literacy practices specific to a particular field of endeavor. We disagree, however, with their view that a linear progression from generic to disciplinary occurs. Instead, we have found that people move in and out of many domains, and the disciplines are not the only specialized domains in which people participate.

Thus, rather than progressing from one basic domain to a given disciplinary domain, all people continually navigate across multiple domains and the literacy practices associated with those domains (Moje, 2013). However, we do acknowledge the uniqueness of literacy practices of highly specialized domains, including the disciplines of science. For example, the abstract nature of scientific texts is partly a result of the text's high degree of lexical density, which is the number of content words within a single clause or sentence (Fang, 2005). These content words are technical vocabularies specific to the discipline. Because the disciplinary literacy practices of a scientist are different from those of a historian, mathematician, poet, writer, or lawyer, students from middle school onward require more advanced skills to be able to read challenging texts in science. The research further implies that teachers outside the discipline (e.g., English teachers, as is often assumed in schools) may not be best equipped to teach those kinds of specialized literacy skills.

LEARNING SCIENCE LITERACY

There is thus a need for the integration of literacy instruction and science content teaching. This synthesis calls for a new approach in conceptualizing science as a unique discourse replete with specialized literacy practices, which students must learn in order to master the knowledge of the discipline. Literacy instruction in science should therefore focus on helping students learn the specific ways of knowing, talking, writing, and doing in science, rather than on learning a set of generic reading strategies for engaging with texts. At the same time, science teaching is not merely about building knowledge in the discipline. It also involves an understanding of how that knowledge is produced. As such, secondary school science requires practices of prediction, observation, analysis, collaboration, and presentation in the construction of accepted and emerging scientific knowledge. All of these practices entail specific demands, such as textual interpretation and verbal and written communication, to be learned before they can be enacted. Most adolescents are not familiar with these practices. Science teachers therefore need to engage students in these practices and make explicit the unique language demands the practices entail.

Learning science literacy is not merely a progression from generic to disciplinary literacy practices but is rather a matter of navigating the many different—often specialized—domains of life (including life inside school). It is thus critical that science teachers help students in that process of navigating from one domain to another and back again. In other words, science teachers need to practice the following:

- Take into consideration young people's interests, knowledge, and text practices.
- Acknowledge the domain-specific nature of those literacy practices (e.g., the literate practices of car enthusiasts can be considered as specialized, like those of scientists).
- Use that domain-specific practice as a basis to teach students the literacy practices of the sciences.

This integration might include helping students navigate the spaces between the practices of home and school language, between the practices of different cultural groups and the sciences, and between the practices of popular media and the sciences. Understanding these various disparities is crucial at a time when the enrollment of science and technology courses in technologically advanced countries is continually falling (Osborne, Simon, & Collins, 2003). Because students often feel disconnected from and put off by the decontextualized and abstract nature of the subject matter, particularly at the secondary level, making a stronger connection between informal and formal learning is crucial in addressing the declining enrollment (Barton, Tan, & Rivet, 2008; Moje & Dillon, 2006; Moje, Peek-Brown, et al., 2004).

The world is also going through a "multimodal turn" in which there is an increasing attention to the importance of nonverbal modes of representation. Although most science educators know that scientific communication involves more than just language, research in science classroom discourse prior to the turn of this century tended to focus on its linguistic and verbal aspects. The phenomenon of multimodality calls attention to the challenges of reading scientific texts that include language, illustrations, charts, and other ways of representing knowledge as crucial to the development of scientific knowledge, skills, and practices. These multimodal literacy practices include not only proficiency in interpreting a single mode of representation, such as reading a graph or making sense of a schematic diagram, but also fluency of translating from one mode to another and combining multiple modes to construct canonical scientific meanings. Research has routinely demonstrated that scientific concepts are constructed through the joint coordination of two or more modes of representation, and it thus follows that science teaching also needs to foreground the role of multimodal literacies (Kress, Jewitt, Ogborn, & Tsatsarelis, 2001; Lemke, 1998).

Given these many perspectives, science educators need to consider how to tap these ideas to improve student academic learning in science. What is the role of literacy, what is the role of disciplinary practice, and what potential do both have for changing teaching practices and for advancing student achievement of the Common Core State Standards (Council of Chief State School Officers, 2010) and Next Generation Science Standards? We hope that the following vignettes, based on our research and experiences as science classroom teachers, will give some insights into these questions.

SCENARIOS

SCENARIO 1: Engaged Reading of Complex Text in the Service of Inquiry[1]

The setting: The setting for this scenario is a middle school science classroom in a large midwestern industrial city. The seventh-grade class is studying biology—and specifically epidemiology—via an inquiry-based unit on communicable diseases, with underlying concepts such as cell structures, the role and function of bacteria and viruses in disease, and the question of how best to study, or track, diseases. Ninety-five percent of the students are African Americans. The majority of the children in the school qualify for the free or reduced lunch rate.

The characters: The characters include Liz Hall and her thirty-two science students.

The context: This context involves a lively group of seventh-grade students who seem to enjoy scientific investigation, but have not learned the practices—including science reading and writing—that support scientific investigation. The students' reading and writing skills vary; some struggle with comprehension and composition in ways that affect their ability to read and write science texts beyond basic levels. For example, when reading, most of the students can recognize and say the words on the page of a text and, in many cases, can comprehend simple facts from a piece of text, but they do not always develop conceptual understandings of the texts they read. The students often read only to complete the task; they do not routinely take information from texts, ask questions of texts, synthesize ideas across texts, or develop new understandings and ideas when they read.

As students explore the phenomenon of communicable diseases, they investigate the subject via experiments in growing bacteria, conducting simulations that track the path of a disease, and reading and writing about the concepts. The goal of the curriculum, in alignment with the Common Core State Standards and Next Generation Science Standards, is to develop scientific thinking, questioning, and communication practices in students.

The dilemma: Although the possibilities for making the abstractions concrete are rich, Liz's students are easily distracted by "seductive details"—those that are interesting without necessarily being relevant (Wade, Schraw, Buxton, & Hayes, 1993)—in both texts and discussions. As well, Liz is struggling to find ways to

- inspire student interest in the abstract concepts of the inquiry curriculum;
- maintain students' engagement, while also taking them into deep learning about abstract concepts such as bacteria or viruses;
- engage students in close reading and writing to support scientific investigation;
- teach learners the necessary scientific reading, writing, and thinking skills to allow them to navigate the demands of the text and the inquiry activities; and
- meet all of these demands in the allotted time, which is dictated by a pacing chart that determines where Liz's learners should be in terms of the state content standards on any given day of the year.

This is a daunting and complex dilemma, indeed!

The "solution": After reading through the curriculum and mapping the activities over her allotted time, Liz realizes that she has to make the concepts come to life, not by personifying them (e.g., Mr. Bacteria meets Ms. Virus), but by providing a problem frame that will make students interested in the question of how bacteria or viruses spread and how they can be controlled and dealt with once an infection spreads. She also needs to improve her students' science literacy skills. She resists, however, approaches that could disconnect science reading and writing from scientific investigation.

Instead, Liz decides to integrate reading, discussion, and writing (secondhand investigation) with hands-on (firsthand) investigation (see Palincsar & Magnusson, 2001) so that they serve as scaffolds for one another. In this way, reading, writing, discussion, and hands-on work all serve as forms of inquiry (Pearson, Moje, & Greenleaf, 2010). Specifically, to start the unit, as part of "bell work," Liz asks the students to spend a few minutes writing in their journals on the question of whether teens under the age of eighteen should be allowed to get tattoos or body piercings without parental consent. As they write, she completes the typical business secondary school teachers must deal with at the start of a class period (e.g., attendance), and then she opens the class with a discussion on the bell-work question. Students are immediately engaged in a rousing debate, although the vast majority of the students feel that parental permission requirements are oppressive and unfair to teens. Liz then concludes the debate and asks the students to read an article she distributes. She instructs them to write an addendum to their bell-work journal entry when they finish reading.

The article reports, in a graphic fashion, on the number of serious bacterial infections people—including adults—routinely experience after receiving tattoos or piercings. The article also reports on the number of people who die as a result of those infections. A hush—punctuated by the occasional "Ugh!" or "Sick!"—falls over the room as students read. A buzz begins to build as students conclude their reading, but Liz reminds them to write before they discuss. After allowing all students to finish reading and writing, she again engages the students in a discussion of the question, advising them to use data from the article to support their claims. The debate takes a dramatic turn; far fewer students argue for unrestricted decision making on the part of teens, although many students persist in their argument, pointing out that even adults succumb to infection, and thus the issue is not about age, but about appropriate care.

After about eight minutes of discussion, Liz launches into the day's lesson: Understanding the key features of bacteria and viruses, how they are alike and different, and how they spread. She works toward this goal by listing the words on the board and then turning to another text reading, this time a very brief newspaper article on a new hospital ruling that nurses will not be allowed to wear any kind of artificial fingernails. The article claims that the rule has been instituted because research shows that bacteria and viruses are more likely to incubate under long, acrylic nails than under shorter, natural nails. Both female and male students look askance at their nails, and several young women with especially long acrylic nails look anxiously around the room at their classmates. Liz asks the students whether they think this finding is accurate and proposes that they do an investigation to determine the validity of the claim. She asks them to write an exit slip to hand her as they leave the room. Each exit slip should include a research question or questions, a hypothesis to be tested, the variables to consider, and a brief description of how they will set up the experiment. The class concludes for the day, with the class prepped to study the growth of bacteria and viruses under the fingernails of various classmates.

In the following days, the students conduct investigations of the question by swabbing fingernails of different lengths, culturing the products of the swabs in petri dishes, and observing and documenting through various modes (drawings, tables, graphs, and prose) whether and how much bacteria grows in those dishes. At the conclusion of this first investigation in the unit, the students write scientific explanations using a claim-evidence-reasoning rubric offered in the curriculum (Moje & Hinchman, 2004; Moje, Peek-Brown, et al., 2004). Liz also uses literacy teaching tools such as a semantic feature analysis chart to examine the common and distinct features of bacteria and viruses. These tools, derived from studies of how people read and write, prove to be invaluable in the curriculum when they are integrated into scientific investigation.

The rationale for the instruction: By integrating reading, writing, discussion, and investigation, Liz addresses the need to teach abstract concepts deeply, but within a tightly specified and constrained time frame. She also works on scientific literacy development by engaging the students in text reading and writing. In particular, she

- gives students opportunities to read and write;
- introduces key vocabulary;
- asks students to consider the differences between two key concepts that will be revisited throughout the curriculum;
- teaches them how to document findings using many different modes of representation;
- frames a problem worthy of investigation through reading, writing, discussion, and firsthand inquiry, which makes the literacy practices of the curriculum scientific and, more important, meaningful, giving students a reason to read closely and to write with precision (Moje & Speyer, in press); and
- connects the abstract concepts to the students' lives and simultaneously expands their worlds by offering them new information, ideas, and knowledge through the reading, writing, and discussion.

In this lesson, the text reading inspires interest, but it also equips students with an introduction to the concepts of bacteria and viruses, as well as to a question for investigation. Too often, teaching practices designed to be "culturally responsive" leave students basking in their already well-developed interests, knowledge, and skills (see Delpit, 1988; Moll & Gonzales, 1994). Instead, Liz's approach recognizes, values, and expands her students' interests, knowledge, and skills.

Questions for Reflection

1. In what ways is Liz teaching science literacy? What aspects of literacy instruction are not being emphasized? What aspects go beyond the typical science classroom?

2. How does Liz use what she knows about her seventh-grade students to make her science curriculum responsive to and expansive for students?

3. Are students learning to be scientific thinkers? How does this instructional approach prepare them to be citizens who can use reading, writing, and discussion to engage in public discourse about science-related issues in everyday life?

SCENARIO 2: Integrating Content Instruction and Disciplinary Literacy Standards in Science

The setting: A public middle school in the suburbs of a major metropolitan area.

The characters: Shannon Farrell, a science teacher with an English minor, is occasionally asked to teach a period or two of English classes. As a result, she attends both English language arts (ELA) and science department meetings. After five years of teaching, Shannon spent four weeks of her summer working at a local National Writing Project (NWP) site to become a NWP Teacher Consultant. During this time, she worked on improving her teaching skills through research on the topic of content area literacy. Shannon's science department is comprised of teachers with varying years of experience with and attitudes toward the many recent changes in the state and national science curriculum.

The context: The ELA department has been reviewing the Common Core State Standards (CCSS) recently adopted by Shannon's state. As Shannon participates in this review, she discovers that there are literacy standards for reading and writing not only in ELA, but also in social studies, science, and technical subjects. Shannon is charged with bringing this information to the members of the science department for discussion and implementation.

The dilemma: Shannon knows that literacy teaching and learning will be a difficult topic to approach with her colleagues in the science department. She expects to hear comments such as "I'm not a reading teacher" or "These standards don't apply to us" as she explains the CCSS to them. To make matters worse, the new Next Generation Science Standards (NGSS) have been recently adopted by her state, and there has already been much debate in the department about the number of these standards and benchmarks. Even so, Shannon feels there may be more "buy in" from the science teachers for the NGSS than for the CCSS because the former were written by scientists and science educators.

The "solution": Shannon knows she must be cautious in her approach with the science department members. As she studies the NGSS, she realizes that they are not separate from the CCSS as she had assumed. Thus, she plans meetings to help her science colleagues see the connection between the two sets of standards. During the first meeting, she shows the teachers the book that provides the foundation of the NGSS: *A Framework for K–12 Science Education: Practices, Crosscutting Concepts, and Core Ideas* by the National Research Council (2012).

Shannon begins the discussion by focusing on eight scientific practices that the National Research Council (2012) agrees are specific to scientists and engineers:

1. asking questions (for science) and defining problems (for engineering),

2. developing and using models,

3. planning and carrying out investigations,

4. analyzing and interpreting data,

5. using mathematics and computational thinking,

6. constructing explanations (for science) and designing solutions (for engineering),

7. engaging in argument from evidence, and

8. obtaining, evaluating, and communicating information.

The teachers agree that students must be able to engage in these practices in order to be successful in any science course. The majority feel comfortable in their instruction of the first five practices but weaker in the last three practices. Shannon points out that scientific knowledge only develops through the actions that scientists undertake in Practices 6 through 8. Shannon shares some examples of her instruction and assessment that include these practices. For instance, in the sixth practice of constructing a scientific explanation, Shannon uses a flowchart to help her students visualize the causal or temporal sequences within the explanation. She then elicits several ideas relevant to the explanation and gets the students to discuss the logical sequence of these ideas. The key, she says, is to identify these practices and make them the focus in the lesson more explicitly.

In the next meeting, Shannon introduces the CCSS to the science teachers. The teachers are able to easily see the parallels between the scientific skills outlined in the *Framework for K–12 Science Education* book and the literacy skills required of a science learner outlined in the CCSS. Many of the teachers realize they need assistance to improve the way they instruct students in terms of reading and writing like a scientist. Subsequently, Shannon is given release time to create professional development training for the science department based on the examples she has used in her lessons. Shannon then plans her training to consist of two one-hour meetings covering reading and writing.

The first meeting highlights the area of reading. Shannon knows that the textbook is rarely a focus in many science classrooms (Heller & Greenleaf, 2007), and the same is true in her school. Many of her science colleagues think that the students' textbook is either too difficult or out of date. As such, they create their own teacher handouts or "packets" for students to take notes in or to fill in the blanks during inquiries into science practices. To help her colleagues see the relevance of reading in science, Shannon provides them with a very difficult research article on the topic of magnetism and asks them to read it and answer a few questions. Shannon then models a think-aloud activity where she gives her thoughts as she is reading the article out loud.

- She stops at regular intervals to ask questions of the content and the purpose of the author as she moves through the reading.
- She frequently monitors her own understanding and questions whether she needs to reread a passage.
- She also carefully reads the captions of the article's figures and graphs and asks how these illustrations are connected to the main text.

Using the think-aloud activity, she discusses with the teachers the reading skills and reasoning processes that are specific to science. They also discuss why it is important to explicitly show science students how scientists engage with printed text.

In the next activity, Shannon gets the teachers to review various grade-level textbooks on the topic of magnetism. This activity is designed to help them recognize that the overall text structures and features in both textbooks are only slightly different. At the lower levels, the information is presented as fact, while at the higher levels, there is more elaboration of the evidences supporting the ideas. There are two reasons why Shannon feels it is important for students to be able to identify specific types of text structures when engaging with text. First, the literature has shown that explicit teaching of text structure awareness can have a positive effect on reading comprehension (Pearson & Duke, 2002). Second, as listed in the *Framework for K–12 Science Education,* one of the eight scientific practices is "engaging in argument from evidence."

The majority of students are not aware of the most important text structure in science, which substantiates claims with evidence from experiments or other inquiries and tests. As such, most students do not see that scientists' explanations of natural phenomena are built through argumentation with supporting experimental data as evidence. This problem is exacerbated by the fact that students rarely question the validity of the material presented in the textbooks. To address this problem, students need to

- interact with a wide variety of text types in order to process the content in different ways,
- analyze conflicting opinions, and
- think critically about how the information is organized and presented.

Shannon shares an approach that relies on the use of out-of-school texts such as news articles, television broadcasts, websites, or Internet videos to augment the textbook. Students can then compare and evaluate why various text structures, vocabulary, and pictorial representations are used in different texts according to varying purposes of the authors and anticipated needs of readers.

The second session that Shannon presents to her department members focuses on writing. In this area, Shannon knows that students do little writing in most science classrooms. Thus, she suggests to the teachers that students should write more often, albeit in small amounts. Their texts could be short summaries of reading passages or videos. Teachers can also ask them to write a caption for a given figure or diagram. For extended writing, Shannon encourages the teachers to give their students at least one writing assignment that includes some independent research and multiple drafts on a suitable topic.

Writing can also be a literacy tool to aid assessment in science. Shannon knows that the majority of the assessments in science lessons contain multiple-choice questions targeted at the lower cognitive levels of Bloom's Taxonomy. She suggests that this problem can be addressed by changing the multiple-choice questions into open-ended questions. As an example, Shannon shares a multiple-choice question that is intended to be used as part of an assessment in a unit on energy conversions. The question, which she takes directly from a textbook, simply asks, "Using the figure below, at what position does the pendulum have zero potential energy?" Shannon explains that she wants to increase the difficulty of the question while also forcing the students to explain their thinking through writing. Thus, she creates the following essay question:

> Jonny sets up a simple pendulum in the laboratory to observe energy conversions that are taking place. Below is the diagram that Jonny draws to represent his experimental setup and laboratory observations. Explain what occurs with the energy conversions as the pendulum moves from Position 1 to Position 5.

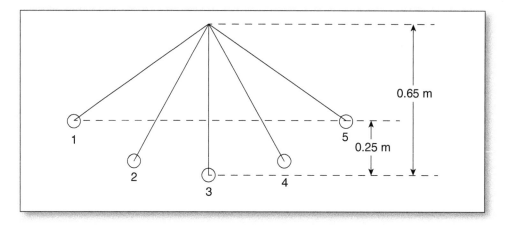

Shannon informs the teachers that many students can correctly explain how energy converts from one form to another (potential to kinetic and vice versa), but they often forget to identify the reference level from which the potential energy is measured. By asking students to answer a more open-ended question through writing, Shannon can better identify the mistakes they have made. This level of detail and nuance is something that teachers cannot achieve with simple multiple-choice questions.

The rationale for the instruction: In sum, the science instruction is focused on helping Shannon's students to read and write like scientists. At the same time, she needs to make sure both her science and ELA students can meet the CCSS for reading and writing when they take the assessments. With much of the current focus on the CCSS for ELA and mathematics as the assessable content, Shannon knows that if students are exposed to the literacy standards in their other classes, it will help their overall performance. Shannon's ultimate goal is to make her students "literate" across all the specialized disciplines.

Questions for Reflection

1. To what extent do you feel that science teachers should be concerned with the Common Core State Standards for literacy in science and technical subjects?

2. What do you think is the main goal of a middle school science teacher? Why do you say so?

3. What are some other possible potential barriers to a successful integration of science content and scientific literacy in your school? How can these barriers be overcome?

4. In Shannon's classroom, she uses a think-aloud approach of instruction to explicitly show her students the literacy practices of science. What role, if any, do you see for this method in your own teaching?

5. How can Shannon make sure that the science teachers continue their focus toward integrating content and scientific literacy in their teaching? How might she follow up this preparation to help the department meet its instructional goals?

SCENARIO 3: Foregrounding Multimodal Literacy Practices in Concept Learning

The setting: An Honors Physics classroom in a suburban high school. The students who enroll in Honors Physics are usually college-bound students who excel in mathematics and science.

The characters: Brad Shelton is one of the few physics teachers in the school's science department. He is very conscientious regarding the way physics concepts must be taught depending on the level of the course as well as the students' abilities. Naomi is a tenth-grade student in Brad's Honors Physics course. She has a positive attitude toward school, is friendly and outgoing, and participates in cheerleading. She is typically an A student and aspires to go to medical school.

The context: An important requirement in the mastery of physics, according to most state and national curricula, is to understand numerous "concepts" of the discipline (Tang, 2011). For instance, the National Science Education Standards (National Research Council, 2012) has a list of science concepts such as force, energy, and interactions for students to master. Students' understanding of these concepts is frequently tested through high-stakes assessments.

The dilemma: Physics is a difficult discipline for many students to master. Students often lament that the concepts in physics are very dense and abstract. Yet, there is little understanding among teachers and students regarding which concepts are central to understanding the discipline of physics. Brad's student Naomi, for instance, describes the conceptual demands of physics by saying that the field requires knowledge of terms,

> like "every action has an opposite and equal reaction." A lot of the definitions have math to back them up. But it's not like normal math where it's like sine of x. It's like weird math. It's like physics and math together. And I feel like there are a lot of concepts that you have to understand, to visualize it in your mind. And this is where I think it's kind of confusing, because if you can't visualize it, then it's hard to understand it.

Due to this confusion about what constitutes a scientific concept, there is a belief that they can be mastered only by those with rare abilities (Lemke, 1990). This belief in the scientific muse explains why many struggling students resign themselves to the belief that they just cannot "get it" when they try to understand the concepts taught in physics. What these students do not realize is that part of the reason why they struggle to "get it" is because the various language and multimodal connections that constitute a concept have not been explicitly taught to them.

The "solution": Brad wants to demystify the common perception of a concept as an idea where students either "get it" or don't "get it." Instead, based on his understanding that a scientific concept is articulated across language and multimodal representations that are depicted according to scientific conventions, he wants to unpack the process of concept learning by foregrounding the various literacy practices involved in any concept. He also stresses the many nuances of language and visualization that students often have difficulty with, and repeatedly gets students to practice translating from one mode to another.

For example, Newton's Laws of Motion are usually taught through a combination of definitions, diagrams, symbolic expressions, numerical calculations, and physical models. Newton's First Law, for instance, is usually introduced to the students as a definition: "An object at rest will stay at rest and an object in motion will stay in motion in a straight line at a constant speed unless acted upon by a net force." Most of the students believe that the ability to recite the definition of Newton's First Law means they can "understand" it. Brad, however, recognizes that there are many interconnected ideas embedded within the definition that require explicit exposition. This interconnected "big picture," rather than the ability to label parts, is what he wants them to understand.

Vocabulary instruction is important in Brad's approach to help students unpack the complex ideas embedded in physics definitions. As such, he introduces a modified version of the Frayer model of vocabulary/concept instruction (Frayer, Frederick, & Klausmeier, 1969). He asks students to create a definition in their own words, rather than rewriting what is in the textbook. He also asks them to give characteristics of the concept, including a list of examples and nonexamples. In addition, he encourages them to include diagrams, symbols, and equations. These activities help students to construct more than a written definition of the concept.

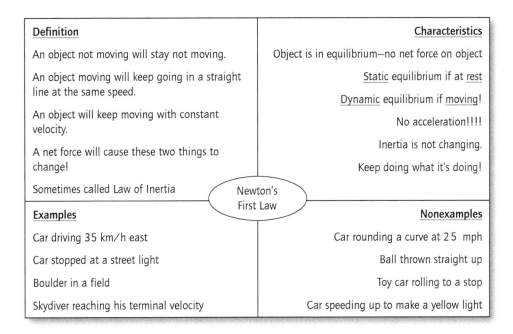

Definition	Characteristics
An object not moving will stay not moving.	Object is in equilibrium—no net force on object
An object moving will keep going in a straight line at the same speed.	Static equilibrium if at <u>rest</u>
	Dynamic equilibrium if <u>moving</u>!
An object will keep moving with constant velocity.	No acceleration!!!!
A net force will cause these two things to change!	Inertia is not changing.
	Keep doing what it's doing!
Sometimes called Law of Inertia	
Examples	**Nonexamples**
Car driving 35 km/h east	Car rounding a curve at 25 mph
Car stopped at a street light	Ball thrown straight up
Boulder in a field	Toy car rolling to a stop
Skydiver reaching his terminal velocity	Car speeding up to make a yellow light

(Newton's First Law)

Although physics is often regarded as a mathematical science, the literacy practices between mathematics and physics are quite different. As Brad teaches Newton's Second Law of Motion, which is often expressed as the mathematical formula $\vec{a} = \dfrac{\vec{F}}{m}$, he knows that a common tendency among students is to substitute given numerical values in the formula to obtain the correct answer. However, the literacy skill required in physics problem solving goes beyond the manipulation of numerical information. It also requires the interpretation of spatial information in a given physical context. For instance, the symbol $\vec{a}$ used to represent acceleration not only is an algebraic symbol that denotes a numerical value; it also conveys a direction in a physical space. This directional aspect is what makes physics a unique discipline.

To represent directional information, physicists use pictorial representations called *free body diagrams* to identify the direction of the forces acting on an object and its resulting motion. Brad knows that many of the students do not use free body diagrams in their problem solving and instead rush to an answer by substituting the given values into the formula of Newton's Second Law. Very often, this approach does not work because the students get the direction wrong. Without the use of a free body diagram, these students are often unable to correctly "picture" the spatial dimension of the physical problem (Tang, Tan, & Yeo, 2011). In this sense, problem solving in physics is a multimodal literacy practice that requires the students to integrate verbal, mathematical, and visual information effectively.

In order for his students to see the multimodal connections in physics problem solving, Brad adopts a procedural and explicit instructional approach to highlight the important literacy steps involved. First, using a think-aloud strategy, he reads the question thoroughly and models how a physicist would think about the information he reads from the question. In particular, Brad often highlights disciplinary words that imply a certain literacy practice in physics that students tend to miss. For instance, the phrase *net force* involves the literacy step of adding different forces acting on an object, which further involves both spatial (through free body diagram) and numerical (through formula) manipulation. As such, Brad will always write the formula on the board and draw the relevant free body diagram if it is absent from the question. Next, he explicitly links the textual, pictorial, and mathematical representations by explaining how he moves from one representation to another. After this modeling, Brad creates many opportunities and assessment tools for his students to practice them.

Last, in order for students to unpack some of the abstract concepts in physics, Brad wants the students to learn about these not only through their textbooks but through their own personal interests and experiences as well. For instance, when Naomi refers to a physics concept as a rule such as "every action has an opposite and equal reaction," she is merely reciting the common definition of Newton's Third Law and has not yet related this definition to her own experiences. Thus, by tapping into the students' area of interest, Brad hopes to create an active and engaging environment where the student can be the expert on a topic (Marzano, Pickering, & Heflebower, 2011). For instance, because Brad recognizes that Naomi knows that cheerleading involves a lot of physics—even if she hasn't made the connections yet—he decides to use cheerleading as an example to teach Newton's Third Law of Motion.

The key idea in Newton's Third Law of Motion is that all forces come in pairs as a result of an interaction between two objects. At a high school level, this process is usually expressed through a mathematical equation such as $\vec{F}_{a\,on\,b} = -\vec{F}_{b\,on\,a}$. Brad knows that many students are not able to comprehend the equation unless they apply it to a part of their common experiences. Thus, using a cheerleading photograph from Naomi, Brad helps the students identify all the interaction pairs of forces and draw a free body diagram of these forces based on their personal experiences. He also asks the students to write down the pairs of forces in both verbal and mathematical form. An example of Naomi's work is shown below.

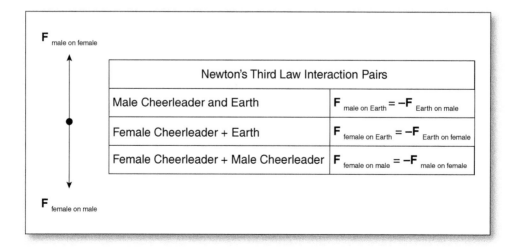

Newton's Third Law Interaction Pairs	
Male Cheerleader and Earth	$F_{male\,on\,Earth} = -F_{Earth\,on\,male}$
Female Cheerleader + Earth	$F_{female\,on\,Earth} = -F_{Earth\,on\,female}$
Female Cheerleader + Male Cheerleader	$F_{female\,on\,male} = -F_{male\,on\,female}$

The rationale for the instruction: Brad's focus throughout his instruction is to make clear that scientists use multiple modes of representations as part of their disciplinary literacy practices. By explicitly showing his students how these multimodal representations are related, he hopes to build their scientific literacy.

Questions for Reflection

1. Think back to a time in school when you had difficulty in a science classroom. What was the concept being taught and why were you having difficulty? What do you think would have helped you do better?

2. How do you know if a student has mastered a scientific concept from your teaching? How do you assess the student's mastery of the concept? Provide an example of an assessment rubric to determine mastery.

3. Brad teaches his students that science is a multimodal discipline. Do you believe one form of representation is better than the others? Provide evidence for your position.

4. Important scientific concepts usually comprise many smaller key ideas. Explain three ways in which a teacher can bridge these key ideas to ensure student mastery of a concept.

5. Brad's instruction focuses on the multimodal representations in a physics classroom. What would these representations look like in a chemistry, biology, or earth science classroom? How are these representations similar and different across the disciplines?

6. What, if any, science literacy practices would be useful in classes across the school curriculum? What literacy practices from other academic disciplines carry over to science classes?

SCENARIO 4: Connecting Hands-on Experiences With Textual Practices

The setting: A two-week summer camp with the objective of teaching basic nanoscience concepts to two classes of seventh graders from a low-income community. The goal of the summer camp is to expose young people to an area currently not mandated in the K–12 science curriculum of most states: nanoscience, the study of atoms, molecules, and other microscopic objects. The summer camp is jointly organized by a large research university, a local educational outreach institution, and the public school district of the students.

The characters: A team of three graduate students, Pedro Ramirez, Kamar Khan, and Kim Schultz, who are tasked to plan and teach a lesson unit called "Size and Scale at the Sub-macro Level."

The context: In designing the lesson unit, the teaching team needs to find ways to integrate several ideas related to nanoscience (e.g., material science, proportional sizes, measurement units) and contemporary biomedical ideas that young people can relate to. This integration is achieved through a "project-based approach" of anchoring the lessons in an interesting real-world scenario of a bacteria outbreak.

The dilemma: The teaching team is cognizant that in a project-based learning approach, they need to provide sufficient hands-on experiential activities, such as designing experiments and using scientific apparatuses, to engage the students' interest. However, given the goal of teaching several concepts of nanoscience, the team also needs to ensure that the hands-on activities do not merely fulfill an engaging role; they must also lead to the development of robust scientific ideas about nano-surfaces. Although the team acknowledges the importance of both hands-on and minds-on activities, they need to find ways to bridge these two aspects of science inquiry instead of treating them as disjointed activities in the overall lesson plan.

The "solution": Pedro, Kamar, and Kim decide that the general approach of each lesson will start with more hands-on activities in dealing with concrete materials and laboratory apparatuses, and progressively introduce more text-based activities that build on those experiences. For the first lesson, after an initial introduction to the bacteria outbreak scenario, the students will perform an experimental task using some sandpapers and salt to simulate different surface textures and bacteria respectively. They will give each group of three students three different grades of sandpaper: fine, medium, and coarse. Students will then put a pinch of salt onto each piece of sandpaper and try to brush the salt off using a piece of paper as a scraper. Given that the fine sandpaper will be the easiest to brush, this experience will provide an analogy to the students that the smooth nano-surface (with surface cracks much smaller than the size of a typical bacterium) will be the most resilient to bacteria residue on its surface. Following this experiential activity, each student will record his or her observation with a drawing in a worksheet before coming together in the group to prepare a poster. Using the poster, each group will present to the class their explanation of what they have observed from their sandpaper experiment.

For the class that first goes through this lesson, Pedro gives a detailed step-by-step instruction to the students on how to carry out the sandpaper experiment. However, when it comes to the task of recording their observation, his instruction becomes brief and open-ended. He simply tells students to "draw what you observe." Consequently, most of the students literally draw a top view of the sandpaper to represent what they see from the top looking down. They also draw several curves and dots to represent the bumps of the sandpaper and the salt residue on it. During the group presentation, most groups explain that because each type of sandpaper is either more or less "bumpier," the grain size determines whether the salt will be harder or easier to brush off. Consequently, the teaching team feels that these explanations are not sufficient, since they do not take into account the sizes of the surface cracks. The team members also think that the student drawings do not help the learners present their arguments in any way.

After the first lesson, Kamar reflects on the instructions Pedro gave to the students. He concludes that the emphasis given to the experiential aspects of the lesson overshadowed the literacy aspects of telling the students what to observe in their experiments, how to write and draw their observations, and how to communicate their findings. In hindsight, the team realizes they have given insufficient thought to the integration of hands-on and minds-on activities in order to provide a holistic approach in ensuring that the students can grasp the concept of nano-surfaces. They also have not provided enough scaffolding to help the students connect their hands-on experiences with the later literacy tasks that mirror scientists' ways of talking, writing, drawing, and representing.

In particular, Kamar realizes that a specific literacy practice, which they have not taught to the students, provides a crucial link in the learners' ability to explain the concept of nano-surfaces. This literacy practice involves a particular way of drawing, from another perspective, a magnified side-view profile of a surface (see Figure 3.1). Such a specialized way of depicting surfaces is commonly found in scientific writing and is missing in the students' explanation. Based on Kamar's reflection, the teaching team decides that for the second class, they need to explicitly demonstrate how to draw a magnified side-view profile and explain why it provides an important way of representing surfaces.

In the revised lesson for the second class, Pedro waits until most groups have finished the sandpaper experiment and then draws and explains a magnified side-view, instructing the students to include this diagram in their group poster and explanation. As a result, there is an improvement in the quality of the students' explanation during

Figure 3.1 A Magnified Side-View Profile of a Rough Surface

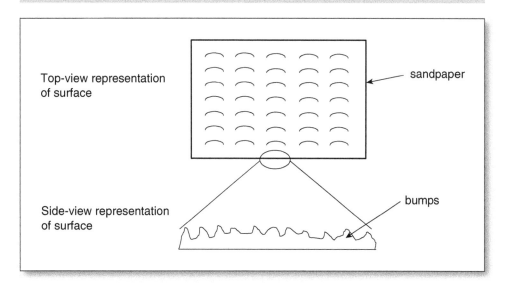

the group presentations due to the use of this diagram. This improvement is evident from the numerous instances where students animatedly gesture at or over the diagram as they explain their reasoning. For example, Mary's group uses their magnified side-view diagrams to show the salt particles residing within the surface cracks of a rough surface. In her explanation, she frequently points at the various peaks, troughs, and salt particles drawn on the poster as she argues, "This surface has bumps that are bigger, so the salt would go right in those cracks. This one has bumps that are much smaller, so the salt won't fit in bumps that small."

Subsequently, with this conceptual understanding facilitated by the use of the side-view visual representation, the second class of students goes on to learn further literacy aspects involved in conceptualizing nano-surfaces, including the quantification of sizes in standardized measurement units (e.g., millimeter, micrometer, nanometer). The side-view visual representation continues to play a crucial mediating role throughout the process as teachers and students frequently use it in their discussions and presentations.

The rationale for the instruction: The team's original lesson plan is based on the general principle that hands-on experiences should provide a basis for the later activities that take on a more text-oriented nature. However, while the broad guiding principle is sound, there is a lack of specificity in thinking about how the hands-on experiences connect to the later textual practices of talking, writing, drawing, and presenting. Without emphasizing this connection, science teachers might focus on the hands-on aspects that usually generate and sustain students' interests in the subject matter, and neglect the process of scaffolding those experiences toward the learning objectives of conceptual understanding.

Kamar's analysis of the gap in the first lesson is informed by his reading of Latour and Woolgar's (1979) work on scientific practices (see chapter introduction). The reading has provided him with relevant insights on how to see the transition from hands-on to minds-on activities as mediated through the role of literacy, or more specifically, multimodal literacies. Instead of viewing an activity as either hands-on or minds-on, Kamar sees every activity as a continual chain of multimodal translations from one mode of representation to another, for example, from manipulating material objects to speaking or scribbling notes, from written notes to drawing or graphing, and so on. Each translation involves a particular literacy operation (e.g., reading, writing, drawing, or acting) that transforms the substance of the inscription, or in the case of the lesson, the students' artifact. Furthermore, each literacy operation is not a generic coding/decoding skill, but is a specialized cultural practice specific to the members of the scientific community. Through this lens, Kamar is able to identify the missing link in the chain of translations that has caused a breakdown in the students' conceptual development toward the concept of nano-surfaces. This missing link comes about because the students are not familiar with the side-view way of representing a surface, which is a specialized literacy practice pertaining to science.

Questions for Reflection

1. To what extent does the process of what the students go through in this project-based learning mirror the way scientists carry out their investigation? What literacy practices are involved in these processes, including those specific to science and those common to other areas of expression and representation?

2. To what extent has the revised instruction helped the students give a better scientific explanation of the observed phenomenon? What is the key factor that contributes to the better explanation, and how, as a teacher, can you help your own students incorporate it into their learning?

3. In what ways has the teaching team integrated literacy with science content learning in the revised lesson?

4. What effects does the teaching approach in the revised lesson have on students' ability to speak and write about science properly?

5. What does the teaching team overlook in deciding to teach this way, and what problems might follow from their decision to teach science in this manner?

6. Does the summer camp setting allow the graduate students to bypass the various standards movements, or do their teaching decisions fit comfortably with mandates facing school-based science teachers?

REFERENCES

Barton, A. C., Tan, E., & Rivet, A. (2008). Creating hybrid spaces for engaging school science among urban middle school girls. *American Educational Research Journal, 45,* 68–103.

Council of Chief State School Officers. (2010). *Common Core State Standards.* Washington, DC: National Governors Association Center for Best Practices.

Delpit, L. D. (1988). The silenced dialogue: Pedagogy and power in educating other people's children. *Harvard Educational Review, 58,* 280–298.

Fang, Z. (2005). Scientific literacy: A systemic functional linguistics perspective. *Science Education, 89*(2), 335–347.

Frayer, D., Frederick, W. C., & Klausmeier, H. J. (1969*). A schema for testing the level of cognitive mastery.* Madison, WI: Wisconsin Center for Education Research.

Heller, R., & Greenleaf, C. (2007). *Literacy instruction in the content areas: Getting to the core of middle and high school improvement.* Washington, DC: Alliance for Excellent Education.

Kress, G., Jewitt, C., Ogborn, J., & Tsatsarelis, C. (2001). *Multimodal teaching and learning: The rhetorics of the science classroom.* London, UK: Continuum.

Latour, B., & Woolgar, S. (1979). *Laboratory life: The construction of scientific facts.* Princeton, NJ: Princeton University Press.

Lemke, J. L. (1990). *Talking science: Language, learning, and values.* Norwood, NJ: Ablex.

Lemke, J. L. (1998). Multiplying meaning: Visual and verbal semiotics in scientific text. In J. R. Martin & R. Veel (Eds.), *Reading science: Critical and functional perspectives on discourses of science* (pp. 87–113). New York, NY: Routledge.

Marzano, R. J., Pickering, D., & Heflebower, T. (2011). *The highly engaged classroom.* Bloomington, IN: Marzano Research.

Moje, E. B. (2013). Hybrid literacies in a post-hybrid world: Making a case for navigating. In K. Hall, T. Cremin, B. Comber, & L. C. Moll (Eds.), *International handbook of research in children's literacy, learning and culture* (pp. 359–372). Oxford, UK: Wiley-Blackwell.

Moje, E. B., Ciechanowski, K. M., Kramer, K. E., Ellis, L. M., Carrillo, R., & Collazo, T. (2004). Working toward third space in content area literacy: An examination of everyday funds of knowledge and discourse. *Reading Research Quarterly, 39*(1), 38–71.

Moje, E. B., & Dillon, D. (2006). Adolescent identities as demanded by science classroom discourse communities. In D. Alvermann, D. Moore, K. Hinchman, B. Waff, & S. Phelps (Eds.), *Reconceptualizing adolescents' literacies: A revision* (pp. 85–106). Mahwah, NJ: Erlbaum.

Moje, E. B., & Hinchman, K. A. (2004). Developing culturally responsive pedagogy for adolescents. In J. Dole & T. Jetton (Eds.), *Adolescent literacy research and practice* (pp. 331–350). New York, NY: Guilford Press.

Moje, E. B., Peek-Brown, D., Sutherland, L. M., Marx, R. W., Blumenfeld, P., & Krajcik, J. (2004). Explaining explanations: Developing scientific literacy in middle-school project-based science reforms. In D. Strickland & D. E. Alvermann (Eds.), *Bridging the gap: Improving literacy learning for preadolescent and adolescent learners in Grades 4–12* (pp. 227–251). New York, NY: Carnegie Corporation.

Moje, E. B., & Speyer, J. (in press). Reading challenging texts in high school: How teachers can scaffold and build close reading for real purposes in the subject areas. In K. Hinchman & H. Thomas (Eds.), *Best practices in adolescent literacy instruction.* New York, NY: Guilford Press.

Moll, L. C., & Gonzalez, N. (1994). Critical issues: Lessons from research with language-minority children. *Journal of Reading Behavior, 26*(4), 439–456.

National Research Council. (2012). *A framework for K–12 science education: Practices, crosscutting concepts, and core ideas.* Washington, DC: The National Academies Press.

Norris, S. P., & Phillips, L. M. (2002). How literacy in its fundamental sense is central to scientific literacy. *Science Education, 87,* 224–240.

Osborne, J., Simon, S., & Collins, S. (2003). Attitudes towards science: A review of the literature and its implications. *International Journal of Science Education, 25*(9), 1049–1079.

Palincsar, A. S., & Magnusson, S. J. (2001). The interplay of first-hand and text-based investigations to model and support the development of scientific knowledge and reasoning. In S. M. Carver & D. Klahr (Eds.), *Cognition and instruction: 25 years of progress* (pp. 152–193). Mahwah, NJ: Erlbaum.

Pearson, P. D., & Duke, N. K. (2002). Comprehension instruction in the primary grades. In C. C. Block & M. Pressley (Eds.), *Comprehension instruction: Research-based best practices* (pp. 247–258). New York, NY: Guilford.

Pearson, P. D., Moje, E. B., & Greenleaf, C. (2010). Literacy and science: Each in the service of the other. *Science, 328,* 459–463.

Shanahan, T., & Shanahan, C. (2008). Teaching disciplinary literacy to adolescents: Rethinking content-area literacy. *Harvard Educational Review, 78*(1), 40–61.

Street, B. V. (1984). *Literacy in theory and practice.* Cambridge, UK: Cambridge University Press.

Tang, K. (2011). Reassembling curricular concepts: A multimodal approach to the study of curriculum and instruction. *International Journal of Science and Mathematics Education, 9,* 109–135.

Tang, K., Tan, S. C., & Yeo, J. (2011). Students' multimodal construction of work-energy concepts. *International Journal of Science Education, 33,* 1775–1804.

Wade, S. E., Schraw, G., Buxton, W. M., & Hayes, M. T. (1993). Seduction of the strategic reader: Effects of interest on strategy and recall. *Reading Research Quarterly, 28,* 93–114.

NOTE

1. This scenario is constructed from data collected across a number of classrooms represented in a large-scale study of inquiry-based science curriculum enactment and scientific literacy development (Moje, Peek-Brown, et al., 2004).The names are pseudonyms and the data representations, although an accurate reflection of the range of classrooms in the study, do not necessarily reflect one actual classroom.

Literacy in the Mathematics Classroom

Linda Hutchison and Jennifer Edelman

Whether you agree with the statement that every teacher is a reading teacher or not, mathematics teachers are being asked with increasing frequency to integrate literacy into their classroom instruction. With the pressures of high-stakes testing, standards and curriculum reforms, and teacher accountability measures, it is not hard to see that mathematics teachers already have their hands full with helping students to understand the structure and content of mathematics. Do they really have time to include content area literacy practices? Or should math teachers be exempt from being reading teachers?

The truth of the matter is that mathematics teachers *are* reading teachers. They are also writing teachers, history teachers, P.E. teachers, art teachers, and teachers of virtually every other discipline. Mathematics as a content area offers multiple and frequent connections to other disciplines. Yet, teachers of mathematics continue to be told to add content area literacy to their already packed schedules. Our goal in writing this chapter is to point out the ways in which mathematics teachers are already integrating literacy in their teaching practice. We do not want to add our voices to the already crowded field demanding that teachers do one more thing. Rather, we plan to show mathematics teachers that literacy practices are valuable and can help their students learn mathematics.

When we redefine *text* to include mathematics, we find that writing and reading do play a large role. For instance, vocabulary and problem solving are part of several other discipline-specific literacies required of students in mathematics. The four scenarios in this chapter demonstrate these principles, showing both what is possible and what is already happening in exemplary mathematics classrooms.

TEXTS, MATHEMATICS, AND CONTENT-AREA LITERACY

Content-area literacy in mathematics requires expanding our definition of text. Traditionally, text has been limited to letters combined to make words, which are then joined together in sentence structures, then paragraphs, and so on. If you agree with this narrow definition, then it is easy to say that students do little reading or writing in mathematics. However, there are unique forms of text found in mathematics classrooms, including

- symbols,
- drawings,
- verbal explanations,
- formal proofs, and
- diagrams, among others.

Teachers often ask students to produce a type of text through acting out a problem situation or using manipulatives to model a mathematical concept. Through the production and reading of these types of text, students may begin to understand new mathematical concepts, deepen their understanding of what they have learned, and demonstrate that knowledge through their solutions to mathematical problems.

WRITING AND CONTENT-AREA LITERACY IN MATHEMATICS

The National Council of Teachers of Mathematics (NCTM, 2000) addresses written communication in their Principles and Standards for School Mathematics (PSSM), recognizing that

> the process of learning to write mathematically is similar to that of learning to write in any genre. Practice, with guidance, is important. So is attention to the specifics of mathematical argument, including the use and special meanings of mathematical language and the representations and standards of explanation and proof. (p. 62)

Writing in mathematics provides students an opportunity to reflect on their work and consolidate their thinking about mathematical concepts. This writing can take many different forms in math class, but it is most recognizable when teachers and students communicate their mathematical thoughts using mutually defined symbols.

READING AND CONTENT-AREA LITERACY IN MATHEMATICS

It is not enough for students simply to be able to produce symbolic representations. They must be able to read and understand them. Reading in mathematics class can range from students "decoding" an equation to reading paragraphs in a textbook to making sense of what a problem is asking. The principles underlying the understanding of a mathematical problem are similar to those that are involved in transactional reading theory (Rosenblatt, 1995), which conceives of reading as a dynamic transaction between the text and the reader. This reader-text relationship does not occur in isolation, however. The processes involved are situated in a social context that provides readers with ground rules that produce expected sorts of readings (Smagorinsky, 2011). For instance, the context of school classrooms suggests that responding to a text with a profane critical response is inappropriate, no matter how authentic that exclamation might be in terms of the reader-text relationship.

Ideally, reading is oriented to the construction of meaning, with the reader infusing the textual symbols with personal and cultural experience evoked from memory. A reading experience involves an

> ongoing cycle of generative and reflective meaning-making that begins with a tentative purpose or expectation that guides the reader when she or he encounters the printed text. The text, consisting of printed signs with the capacity to act as symbols, calls up in the reader past experiences, feelings, and images that the reader organizes and synthesizes to create a tentative framework that may be revised, rethought, or rejected as the event proceeds. Each reading event is unique. (Borasi, Siegel, Fonzi, & Smith, 1998, p. 278)

The same could be said for a mathematical problem-solving episode. Students should be both generative and reflective when devising a solution strategy. The purpose for reading is set: The student is reading to find the information necessary to solve the problem. The student brings his or her previous experiences to bear when planning a solution, creating a variety of solution strategies for the same problem. The student is a partner in the problem now, creating a role of authorship for himself or herself.

A transactional view of problem solving in mathematics may lead students and teachers to view mathematics instruction as a place that offers opportunities for authorship and meaning-making. This view would change representations in mathematics from objects that place students in compliant roles, responding to "anonymous commands to perform an operation or solve a particular problem" (Wilson, 2011, p. 438), to more active agents in understanding mathematical operations.

LITERACY IN MATHEMATICS: MORE THAN VOCABULARY

When looking for lesson plans on integrating content area literacy practices in mathematics, teachers often find lessons where vocabulary activities such as making a flip chart of definitions are added to a mathematics lesson. However, literacy practices in mathematics should be thought of as much more than learning vocabulary in isolation. Literacy practices in mathematics, as in other subjects, must have a meaningful intent.

Mathematical English (ME) has a distinctive vocabulary that shares many words with Ordinary English (OE) (Shuard & Rothery, 1984). The difference is that words in ME often have drastically different meanings from those in OE. For example, the word *plane* can be found in both ME and OE, embodying different meanings in each. Students in math classes may be confused when they encounter the term because they think of the OE meaning rather than the mathematical one. This potential confusion accounts for why it is critical to teach vocabulary in context in mathematics. Without context, students will continue to have misconceptions about the meanings of ME words and will find themselves unable to use more formal mathematical vocabulary.

We have observed mathematics classrooms where teachers assign vocabulary activities such as crossword puzzles to help their students learn the mathematics terminology they will need for the current unit they are studying. Students are asked to memorize definitions and then are expected to be able to accurately use those terms when communicating their solutions. However, as with all things, the teaching of vocabulary should begin by connecting the new (formal mathematics vocabulary) with the known (a student's informal vocabulary). Teachers should be explicit in explaining the differences between OE and ME terms, especially when they share a word such as *face* or *mean*. Students need multiple opportunities to practice using ME in context (not crossword puzzles), such as when explaining a solution strategy or making sense of a problem.

In this way, teachers can introduce students to the authentic practices of mathematicians: precise communication where each word is chosen for a specific reason and where the ideas are presented succinctly.

PROBLEM-SOLVING LITERACY

Problem solving is an integral literacy in learning mathematics in that it is central to thinking within and about mathematics. Problem-solving skills enable learners to approach new problems strategically and with confidence that they can find a solution path, even if much about the problem is unfamiliar. George Polya's (1945) problem-solving heuristic predominates most mathematics textbooks. This routine includes the following:

1. Understanding the problem

2. Devising a plan

3. Carrying out the plan

4. Looking back

Each step of Polya's heuristic includes a series of questions that students may ask of themselves to arrive at a solution. For example, in *understanding the problem,* questions include "What is the unknown? What are the data? What is the condition?" (Polya, 1945, p. xvi). When students learn to use these questions strategically, they gain ways to think about problems and to figure out what is being asked—skills that are useful for a lifetime.

Polya's four strategies also offer a way of remembering questions within each step for solving problems. Included in Polya's work is a dictionary that can be used to see how mathematicians read terminology with an expanded context. In mathematics classrooms, teachers and fellow students can model how these questions apply to the specific problems at hand. The goal is to teach these procedures so that students may metacognitively approach problems with fluency and the appropriate use of strategies and formulas. That is, students may "learn to learn" how to solve problems by understanding productive thought processes. The more advanced the problems that students are solving, the more advantageous it is for them to have developed this critical literacy.

NUMERICAL LITERACY

Understanding the relative size or amount of a number is another critical literacy for students. For instance, they must comprehend the positional nature of our symbol system known as place value, which distinguishes 1,000 from 100. Specifically, students need to realize that zeros and ones have different meanings when they are in different places. One thousand dollars is ten times one hundred dollars, preferably in your pocket. Students also need to be able to talk about relative size with understanding. For example, understanding that the unit is in kilometers instead of miles makes a 5-K race time different from a 5-mile race time, even if the runner has a consistent stride.

NUMBER LINE LITERACY

The number line is one of the first tools students learn to use in elementary mathematics, and it continues to be useful throughout their school mathematics experiences. It is important that students become literate with this tool. But what exactly is number line literacy? What does it look like at the elementary, middle, and high school levels?

Number lines in elementary school. A number line may seem to be a self-explanatory tool. After all, it looks like the picture below.

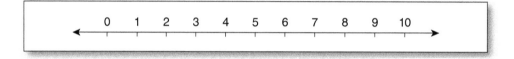

Young children quickly see that this is a list of numerals that is presented in a familiar, linear order. Teachers can readily show students how to use the tool for counting, addition, and subtraction.

Number lines also continue to be an important tool in the middle grades, as the intervals can be increased to include common fractions and decimals. Using a number line at this stage will help students visualize how there are numbers that are *between* whole numbers. Again, a number line can help students compare and order fractions and decimals as well as perform addition and subtraction with parts of whole numbers.

Number lines in middle and high school. Number lines are a powerful way to show students the position of negative numbers in relation to the counting numbers they have become comfortable using. Such a number line would look like the picture below.

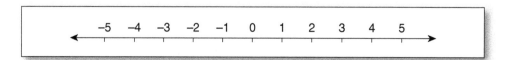

Here, the number line is a useful model for addition and subtraction with integers, given that students can physically manipulate objects on a number line as well as draw the steps taken in these operations.

SPATIAL LITERACY IN MATHEMATICS

Building on their familiarity with number lines, students in Grades 7 through 12 can begin graphing functions in algebra. Because they have become fluent with a number line where negative values are to the left and positive values are to the right, they are able to translate that experience to a Cartesian plane by adding a second number line vertically where negatives are below the x-axis and positive values are above. By using a visual model such as a number line, students are able to reason spatially to ask themselves if their graph makes sense. The ability to read a coordinate graph, which is critical not only for mathematics but also for science, is a key aspect of spatial literacy that students put into practice in everyday life. It requires a notion of function and the ability to translate the data from the graph into a story of what it is telling the reader.

Students also use spatial reasoning daily in situations such as time and location. The ultimate question we would like students to be able to answer for themselves in terms of spatial reasoning is this: How do things fit together? A real-world example of spatial reasoning—or, more specifically, the consequences of the lack of it—involves a driver's overreliance on his or her GPS when driving in an unfamiliar place. Recently, a woman and her daughter followed their GPS onto a back road in Death Valley, ran out of gas, and ended up severely dehydrated and near death as they tried to hike out. When instructed to turn off a paved road for an unpaved road, the driver might have questioned the GPS instructions. Had they asked themselves if their mental (or paper) maps fit with what the GPS was telling them to do, they might not have ended up in such a dire situation. To be spatially literate, students must be able to reason logically and determine if their answers (or directions, in the case of a GPS) are reasonable.

Spatial reasoning also requires the ability to visualize a three-dimensional figure when it is represented in two dimensions. Many people who claim not to be mathematically literate actually engage in such operations every day. For example, architects and designers may use a two-dimensional scale floor plan to represent a building or room in a house; people with spatial literacy have the skills required to take these plans a step further and actually picture the room, while others cannot visualize these spatial relations (Smagorinsky, Cook, & Reed, 2005). Spatial literacy is also important for students in calculus courses, where they need to be able to picture resulting figures when something spins around something else. It is the only way problem solvers can figure out what mathematical operations should be employed to find out a volume or surface area.

GRAPHING LITERACY

Another important literacy in mathematics deals with not only coordinate graphing but also reading tables and graphs for data. It is important for students to be able to discern what a graph is actually representing about real-life phenomena and to be able to decide which type of graph best represents a data set.

Teaching children about reading a graph begins early in K–12 schooling when they learn how to look at a Venn diagram to organize sets of things. When the kindergarten teacher has a student sign in for lunch by putting her name in a hula hoop to indicate which entrée she is choosing, the child is beginning to learn set theory through the use of a graphing model.

Students also need to be taught to recognize that it's possible to misrepresent conclusions about data in creating a graph (Huff, 1954). Whether the task involves reading a politician's graphics to decide how to vote, or learning about hybrid cars via a comparison chart of their miles-per-gallon consumption, reading a graph is a critical literacy taught in mathematics for functioning in society.

STATISTICAL LITERACY

Understanding statistics is a literacy that involves processing information that many students have not been trained to consider automatically. Huff (1954) provided several questions to evaluate statistical reports when a specific statistic is cited, such as "Who says so?" For example, students doing research on the consequences of cigarette smoking might check cigarette manufacturers' data or the American Cancer Society data—and find completely different information. In addition to asking "Who says so?" students should also be taught to ask, "How do they know?" This question allows them to interrogate the means by which a conclusion has been reached so that they may evaluate the verity of the claims. A third essential question is "What's missing?" This attention ensures that students don't miss "the fine print" as they evaluate how a claim is supported. For instance, students might read a report that states that one out of three high school seniors scored a 36 on the ACT in a given graduation year. Unless students address the issue of what's missing, they will not realize that the school's enrollment of seniors was limited to three people.

"Did somebody change the subject?" is another good question teachers can prompt students to consider as they look at statistics, because data can prove startling when information has never been collected previously and comparisons are assumed nonetheless. For instance, reports of "increasingly high scores on the ACT" might be suspect if prior ACT scores are not available. The most important question Huff lists is this: "Does it make sense?" This question might have helped the stranded drivers who relied on the GPS system, even when its coordinates did not match the disconfirming evidence available through their own observations.

MODELS/MODELING USING SYMBOLS

Critical literacy in mathematics involves reading symbols that have their own meaning system, one that is different from how they might be interpreted in other contexts. Students must be taught to read the symbols in mathematics so that meaning can be ascribed. Many mathematical symbols describe an operation or a relationship. For example, the dash for a mathematician is a subtraction symbol or a negative or inverse. Not only would the same symbol mean something quite different in a strictly verbal context, but also the mathematics student must understand the context of the symbol to determine its meaning in a mathematical operation.

Other symbols are less ambiguous among mathematicians, yet potentially esoteric to the novice student. For instance, an experienced mathematics student knows to read $C = \pi d$ as "the circumference is equal to *pi* times the diameter," a formula that holds for all circles. The modeling of reading a symbol system is an important part of teaching mathematics. Students need to hear and read how the symbol systems are expressed.

Another aspect of using symbols occurs when models are used to represent a physical situation. For instance, it is important to many mathematicians and scientists to be able to create a reasonable model for the stream flow of a river. These models involve equations that will show how variables are related in an equation or expression and, in a sense, suggest a narrative for how a process unfolds. Mathematics problems often involve students in the task of identifying the proper integer for a missing variable in a formula, from $x + 3 = 6$ to something like "If $\frac{1}{2}x + \frac{1}{2}(\frac{1}{2}x + \frac{1}{2}(\frac{1}{2}x + \frac{1}{2}(\frac{1}{2}x + \ldots = y$, then $x = ?$" Most modeling applications in higher-level science require students to fit data into an unknown equation to figure out how an equation can best model the real-world phenomenon.

TECHNOLOGY

Mathematics uses technology in ways that are different from how it is used in other content areas. Not only is it necessary for students to understand calculators in mathematics, but also microworlds such as dynamic geometric software provide situations in which Euclidean and non-Euclidean geometries can be explored. Students also need to learn how to read spreadsheets and work with programming robots and specific computer languages. It is important for students to have the literacy of understanding the technology tools available for performing tasks in mathematics and translating these results in a meaningful fashion.

PROOF

Mathematics is constructed through specific logical systems in which ideas are justified using an ordered sequence of axioms, definitions, and propositions that, once justified, can be expanded upon for future ideas. The availability of Euclidean and other geometries suggests how mathematics serves as a unique discipline with specific literacy demands. Polya (1945) explains the role of proofs within these practices:

> Now, the system of geometry is cemented with proofs. Each proposition is linked to the foregoing axioms, definitions, and propositions by a proof. Without understanding such proofs we cannot understand the essence of the system.
>
> In short, if general education intends to bestow on the student an idea of logical system, it must reserve a place for geometric proofs. (p. 217)

Grasping the construct of a proof is therefore a central literacy in secondary school mathematics. Proof is a central focus for demonstrating an understanding of the logic of an idea in mathematics and how it fits into an established system.

SCENARIOS

SCENARIO 1: A Learning Community

The setting: Lincoln High School, which serves about a thousand students, is located in a suburban university setting. Most of the students plan to continue their education beyond high school. The university serves as the main employer in town, and most parents either work at the university, own local ranches or businesses, or take graduate classes at the university. Income levels reflect these populations. The school population has Department of Education disaggregate descriptors of 60 percent European American, 20 percent African American, 15 percent Latino/a, 4 percent mixed race, and 1 percent Asian American. Most students at Lincoln High take four years of mathematics in order to meet state graduation standards and to qualify for state-scholarship monies to attend college.

The characters: Peter Johnson teaches both sections of AP calculus, each of which enrolls just under thirty students. He is a very experienced mathematics teacher who has earned a master's degree in mathematics. All of his students have successfully completed the prerequisite mathematics courses (through pre-calculus).

The context: During the first few weeks of school, Peter sets up a classroom ethos establishing a cultural norm that all students are expected to learn and to help one another with their learning. His classroom practices are well established, and many students arrive knowing what is expected of them. He is explicit about his expectations that students who help each other learn can learn more themselves. Consequently, students collaborate on the problem solving that comprises a large part of the normal classroom conversation.

Peter explicitly emphasizes the metacognitive level of questions in choosing strategies for problem solving, with multiple solution paths considered during class. Almost every day, he calls students to the board in groups to work collaboratively on a problem. Students call on others for assistance on the work they are doing, and they help others until everyone arrives at a solution. Peter then calls on students to explain the different strategies they used to arrive at their answer. If a student appears stymied, the teacher expects classmates to provide assistance without stigmatizing those in need of help. Peter thus fosters a positive learning environment focused on learning the ideas together.

When a student is stuck, peers usually ask questions in their response:

"Did you try . . . ?"

"Have you thought of . . ."

Others use words of encouragement such as "I was stuck there too until I remembered . . ."

When students ask Peter a question, he typically refers it to another student who he believes understands the problem. He uses the board work to emphasize the variety of strategies that will work in solving a problem, and he demonstrates a "foolproof" strategy (one that will usually work) by highlighting a student's work from the board in a positive manner. Class members rarely use competitive phrases about scores and so forth in this "everyone benefits when we all learn" model.

The dilemma: A new student, Hugh, joins the class at mid-semester. Hugh has recently moved to the area from one of the state's larger districts, where he had been doing very well in their competitive calculus class. Hugh's mother challenges him with mathematics competition questions at home, and she reinforces Hugh's success in learning by asking how his grades compare with others in the class. Hugh is not used to explaining how he solves problems, and in Peter's class, he just wants to know the "correct" way to solve them in the quickest timeframe possible, preferably before anyone else has finished. Not only does he get frustrated, but he also does not pay attention when his fellow students are at the board or when Peter explores the different strategies that the students have used to solve a problem.

The "solution": Peter approaches the problem in a manner consistent with his personality in the classroom.

1. He talks with Hugh outside class about the importance of problem-solving strategies and the questions students must consider when doing calculus. He explains that these questions will be very helpful to Hugh during mathematics contests and that by listening to others and analyzing his own work, Hugh can improve himself. Peter also emphasizes that by teaching others, Hugh will find that his own work is easier to remember, because the process of explaining a concept helps to reinforce it for the person doing the explaining. During class, Peter continues to positively reinforce the classroom ethos established earlier in the semester.

2. In constructing groups for group work, Peter considers whom to partner with Hugh until he has learned to perform in the established classroom environment. He finds students who will not be intimidated by Hugh's assertions about mathematics and a group that Hugh can work with and learn from as well as teach. He helps Hugh understand the teamwork ethos and fit into the classroom group. Peter changes these groupings frequently so that Hugh can understand the peer perceptions and so that no single group is tasked with changing Hugh's perceptions. Peter is subtle in his approach to convincing Hugh that he will learn by listening as well as by helping others. Peter knows it will take time.

3. He explains his philosophy of learning to Hugh's mother and gives her data on his students' success rate on the AP exam and the next college calculus class, hoping to allay any fears she has about the different approach.

4. He continues to ensure that Hugh gets positive feedback when he helps others and when he asks for help. Peter also positively reinforces Hugh when he provides a good explanation and when he tries something that is different when problem solving. Peter reinforces appropriate use of mathematical language in Hugh's explanations.

The rationale for the instruction: Peter has several reasons for choosing the teaching strategies he employs. He sees that having students work collaboratively reduces the anxiety that students feel in solving problems because the atmosphere is supportive. He also believes that the supportive atmosphere will also serve to reduce test anxiety on the AP exam. He recognizes that by requiring students to explain their problem-solving strategies, he ensures that the other students are exposed to different approaches. This distribution of authority also allows him to assist students with mathematical language and with their thinking about both the calculus and the problem solving. He believes that students who explain their thinking in the manner of a teacher learn and reinforce their ideas. And, because the process of making thinking explicit is part of the classroom conversation, Peter can moderate these ideas and speech and make them more appropriate to the expectations for mathematical discourse. By reinforcing a variety of solution strategies, Peter encourages students to understand how things are working instead of reinforcing a single-strategy model.

Peter's teaching approach mirrors a mathematician's approach to problem solving. A professional mathematician works in a community where mathematical ideas are discussed and where the give and take of these ideas is both valued and expected. By providing these sorts of discussion opportunities to his students, Peter is affording them an opportunity to participate in the mathematical literacy he is teaching. He respects his students as mathematicians and learners, and he ensures that they develop the skills they will need for future mathematical learning.

Questions for Reflection

1. What has Peter foregrounded in teaching how to go about problem solving?

2. To what extent has his instruction helped prepare students to perform well on standardized tests?

3. In what manner, if at all, does Peter's approach prepare his students to meet the Common Core State Standards?

4. How effectively has Peter taught so as to provide his students with an authentic literacy experience?

5. What effects does Peter's teaching approach have on students' ability to speak and write properly?

6. What is the likelihood that Peter's teaching will benefit students' literacy in future mathematics classes?

7. What is the likelihood that Peter's teaching will help students do well academically in their courses across the high school curriculum? In future mathematics courses?

8. What does Peter overlook in deciding to teach this way, and what problems might follow from his decision to teach mathematics literacy in this manner?

9. If you were evaluating him as an administrator, how would you assess his teaching?

SCENARIO 2: Extended Responses on Standardized Tests

The setting: Roosevelt Middle School is the only public middle school serving a small, rural town, but it is part of a larger countywide school district. The school serves students in Grades 6 through 8, pulling students from three local elementary schools. The demographics of the school include 63 percent European American, 14 percent African American, 10 percent Native American, 6 percent Latino/a, 1 percent Asian American, and 6 percent other. Eleven percent of students are enrolled in Special Education programs, and 63 percent of students qualify for free or reduced-price lunch.

The characters: Renee Anderson joined Roosevelt Middle School immediately after receiving her teaching credentials. She teaches sixth-grade math to four different groups of students each day. Each class has about thirty students in it.

The context: Roosevelt Middle School has failed to make Adequate Yearly Progress (AYP) for the past three years and has been labeled as "failing" by the state. Normally, this designation would allow students to move to another school of their choice, but because Roosevelt is the only middle school in the town, most remain at the school. The testing window will begin in three weeks, and the principal has identified math as one area that must improve. In this state, a school labeled as "failing" for more than two years in a row can be taken over by outside governance, and all of the teachers could find themselves out of a job if the state determines that a clean start is necessary. Students are under pressure to perform as well. In order to move from eighth grade to high school, students must meet or exceed all math and reading standards on the test.

The dilemma: Under pressure to raise scores for all students, the teachers in the mathematics department examine the prior year's scores to determine which areas they should emphasize to improve all students' performance. The item analysis shows that students score lowest on extended response items. The team brainstorms possible reasons for these scores and decides that students have struggled with writing mathematically. Renee has been assigning extended response problems as homework each week, but she has not seen much improvement in her students' answers. With only three weeks until testing begins, she must find a way to continue covering content as well as practicing extended response problems in the classroom. How can she balance both goals without overwhelming her students?

The "solution": While Renee continues to teach her math content, she decides to integrate the following ideas in her classes over the next three weeks in order to prepare students for the standardized tests.

1. Math journals: Because writing in mathematics class is a challenge for her students, Renee makes mini-journals by folding over several sheets of lined notebook paper and stapling them together at the fold. This tool provides students with a smaller space to "fill up" with their thoughts. She decides to dedicate the last ten minutes of each class session to writing in journals. To spark students' thinking, she comes up with the following prompts:

   o Describe what you learned in math class today.
   o Make a connection between something you learned today and something you learned earlier.

- o Give an example of where you might use what you learned today in the real world.
- o Imagine you are teaching today's concept to a younger student (fourth or fifth grade). What would you tell them is the most important thing about _____?

2. Analyzing exemplars: Renee scours the Internet for sample student papers for extended response items. She gives each of her students a copy of the grading rubric for extended response items used by the company that administers the standardized test and asks them to grade the sample papers. At first, many of the students mark all of the samples as "exceeds standard" because they believe that if a paper has been published online, then it must be good. Renee leads class discussions to see if everyone agrees with these grades, and students soon learn to look more critically at the sample responses.

3. Picture problem solving: The teacher gives students a set of five extended response problems and asks them to choose one to solve. The catch is that they cannot use any equations in their solution. Rather, they must solve the problem using pictures alone. With a partner, each student shows and explains his or her pictures, and the students decide if the problem has been solved accurately and if the explanation makes sense.

4. Partner problem solving: Renee assigns an open-ended problem for homework. The next day, students join groups of four and share their responses. All of the students in each group are held responsible for making sure they understand each other's solutions. The group decides which solution they want to present to the class, and someone other than the person who contributed it must explain it.

The rationale for the instruction: The students' low scores on extended response items may stem from an inability to communicate mathematically. Each of the described literacy activities engages a different communication act. In using math journals, students communicate through verbal texts, but the focus of their writing is not on explaining how to perform a certain algorithm. Rather, the focus is on describing a personal experience in mathematics, making connections between other concepts or events that the students have experienced, and taking on the role of a more knowledgeable peer to explain a concept in words that others would understand. These are all important parts of what it means to do mathematics, what Moje (2008) terms "disciplinary literacy," which "builds an understanding of how knowledge is produced in the disciplines, rather than just building knowledge in the disciplines" (p. 97). A focus on how knowledge is generated in mathematics is a goal of disciplinary literacy. This generation of mathematical knowledge, Moje proposes, "operates according to particular norms for everyday practice, conventions for communicating and representing knowledge and ideas, and ways of interacting, defending ideas, and challenging the deeply held ideas of others in the discipline" (p. 100).

Using exemplars will help students develop a critical eye, and the class as a whole will begin to define for itself exactly what constitutes proof. Renee shows the students what the state considers to be proof, but then allows her students to extend and amend that definition to meet their own needs. This approach mirrors the actions of any professional mathematical group as they work on problems together and share solutions, while both challenging and defending their ideas. Disciplinary literacy is in action during this activity as students learn what counts as an acceptable explanation for a solution and come to consensus on a definition of proof. The partner problem-solving activity extends the students' exploration of what constitutes proof by having them engage in personal explanations of solutions. They continue to act as mathematicians as they share their solutions and defend their ideas.

The use of pictures to solve problems engages students in a way of conceptualizing mathematics that may be unfamiliar to them. Using pictures may encourage some students to try different solution paths, ones they may not have been able to express using symbols and formulas. The pictures allow the students to communicate their thoughts informally. Renee hopes that as students become more comfortable with drawing their solutions, they will also develop a sense of how to most effectively communicate through pictures, which is one of the extended response requirements.

Questions for Reflection

1. What has Renee foregrounded in teaching how to respond to extended response items?

2. To what extent has her instruction helped prepare students to perform well on standardized tests?

3. How effectively has Renee taught so as to provide her students with an authentic literacy experience?

4. What effects does Renee's teaching approach have on students' ability to perform on extended response items and in the class?

5. What is the likelihood that Renee's teaching will benefit students' literacy in future mathematics classes?

6. What is the likelihood that Renee's teaching will help students do well academically in their courses across the middle school curriculum?

7. What does Renee overlook in deciding to teach this way, and what problems might follow from her decision to teach mathematics literacy in this manner?

8. If you were evaluating her as an administrator, how would you assess her teaching?

SCENARIO 3: Geometry and Technology—Why Do We Do Proofs?

The setting: Legacy High School is in a suburb of a large metropolitan area. It is located eight miles from the city center. There are three high schools in the district, and all schools have been built since 1960. The demographics of the school described by the U.S. Department of Education are 52 percent European American, 20 percent African American, 19 percent Latino/a, 4 percent Asian American, and 4 percent two or more races.

The characters: Tracy Grey has taught at Legacy High School for the past five years. She enjoys the access to technology that is available at the school, and it was a deciding factor in her choice of mathematics teaching jobs. She teaches two Geometry classes as well as three Algebra II courses. The students in her classes have used graphing calculators and the TI-Navigator system as part of their Algebra I coursework. She employs graphic representations as another way to envision a concept, a technique she had used in college.

The mathematics department at Legacy High School uses technology as a tool for learning, and all courses are integrated with technology. The department works to keep up with available technologies and use them to enhance their students' learning. If Tracy has math-specific technology questions, she usually can work them through with her fellow teachers. Textbooks and the attendant programs are available online for students to use in and out of school. Students have access to Wi-Fi while at the school throughout the day.

Tracy shares her department's beliefs and philosophy about using technology as a tool for learning. She uses technology to help students have easier access to graphical representations. She regularly schedules the computer lab so that she can work with different dynamic geometry software programs. She wants her students to have visual images of the ideas she is teaching in Geometry, because she believes that students need to envision the problems to really understand the ideas. She wants the image to be moveable so that students can consider different aspects of the visual.

One idea that she considers in this college-preparatory course is the notion of what constitutes a proof in mathematics. While not all students who take the course are headed to a university immediately after high school, most will be going on to college or technical school. Students in the class have varying mathematics backgrounds, and so Tracy finds herself working at many levels, since the course is open to freshmen heading toward calculus as well as seniors taking their last mathematics course.

The context: Students have been working throughout the first semester and have been using a dynamic geometry program to illustrate their work. For the most part, students are comfortable doing the tasks on the computer and are working along with the textbook supplement workbook for the program. Each lesson in the workbook asks for a conjecture about the idea being studied. Students are able to make predictions about the idea and can write and discuss reasonable inferences. They can test their conjectures using the dynamic geometry software, check their veracity using the images and calculating tool, and then decide if their conjectures have merit.

The dilemma: Tracy has the students work through an activity using the dynamic geometric software to demonstrate a variety of proofs of the Pythagorean Theorem.

Each group is assigned to use an existing proof and explain the proof to their fellow classmates. During the presentations, it becomes obvious to Tracy that the students do not understand what constitutes a proof. They are comfortable just following the directions to construct the image, but they do not think through what it means to prove something. Tracy decides that this shortcoming is something she needs to rectify.

The "solution": Tracy decides to undertake several strategies.

1. She begins by having students investigate logical arguments using sentences. She uses the terminology of logic to help construct the veracity of the statements. She specifically teaches the difference between an inductive and deductive proof and begins to have students write both paragraph and two-column proofs from their text. She begins to highlight proofs in the text as well as proofs on the board.

2. She has students use their journals to describe what constitutes a proof versus a supposition or conjecture. She encourages them to provide real-world examples.

3. She has students develop proofs in groups and then work independently so they learn how to construct a proof.

4. She uses the dynamic geometry software to have students construct the model with the givens and then write a paragraph proof or two-column proof in a text box with animation for the steps.

The rationale for the instruction: Tracy undertakes to develop her students' under-standing of a proof versus a conjecture because she wants them to be able to reason like a mathematician. She realizes that mathematics beyond her class will depend on an adequate understanding of both proof and logic. She wants students to be able to recognize fallacious arguments and assertions. Tracy feels this grasp of the chain and transit of logical thinking is an important democratic literacy that is developed in using mathematics well.

Questions for Reflection

1. What has Tracy foregrounded in teaching how to go about proof?

2. To what extent has her instruction helped prepare students to perform well on standardized tests?

3. In what manner, if at all, does Tracy's approach prepare her students to meet the Common Core State Standards?

4. How effectively has Tracy taught so as to provide her students with an authentic literacy experience?

5. What effects does Tracy's teaching approach have on students' ability to speak and write properly?

6. What is the likelihood that Tracy's teaching will benefit students' literacy in future mathematics classes?

7. What is the likelihood that Tracy's teaching will help students do well academically in their courses across the high school curriculum?

8. What does Tracy overlook in deciding to teach this way, and what problems might follow from her decision to teach mathematics literacy in this manner?

SCENARIO 4: Evidence of Content-Area Literacy Practices

The setting: Ames Middle School is a public school located in a large, urban school district consisting of 139 different schools, 89,500 students, and 6,500 teachers. The school itself has 1,045 students, with the following demographics: 40 percent African American, 40 percent European American, 10 percent Asian American, and 10 percent Latino/a. Thirteen percent of students qualify for free or reduced-price lunch, while 9.3 percent of students are enrolled in Special Education programs and 2.1 percent of students are English Language Learners.

The characters: Anita Marvin has been teaching eighth-grade Algebra at Ames for ten years. She holds a master's degree in education from the local university and has a bachelor's degree in both mathematics and secondary education. The principal at Ames retired over the summer, and a new principal, Dr. Anthony Nelson, has been hired. Anthony received his administrator's license days before being hired to lead Ames.

The context: Ames Junior High School is a high-performing school that makes AYP yearly. Test scores remain stagnant, however, and there is a push to get even more students to meet or exceed the standards. As a result, the school leadership is pressured by the district's main office to employ "research-based teaching practices" in order to raise the test scores. One such initiative is the push for content area literacy in all classrooms. To ensure that these initiatives are being implemented, each principal is required to observe every teacher monthly and report to the district office which teachers are using the mandated techniques and which ones are not.

The dilemma: The principal recently observed one of Anita's classes and then sent her the following email shown in Figure 4.1.

After reading this message Anita feels angry, because she knows that she used appropriate content area literacy practices during the lesson her principal observed. The two suggestions he makes (KWL charts and anticipation guides) would not have helped her students learn during her lesson. She also knows that her students were reading and writing during the lesson. Anita needs to find a way to define content area literacy in mathematics so the district and her principal recognize that she is both doing what is best for her students and meeting the district requirements.

Figure 4.1 Observation Feedback Email

From: Anthony Nelson, Ed.D.

Subject: Observation Feedback

Date: 10/24/12

To: Anita Marvin

Ms. Marvin,

As you know I recently completed an observation in your 4th period Algebra class. Overall, the class was well organized, the students were well behaved, and the lesson was engaging.

I do have one concern, however. Our professional development days this year have been spent learning about content area literacy practices. I did not observe any of these practices in your class. I was specifically looking for things such as the use of KWL charts or anticipation guides. I also did not observe any of the students reading or writing during class.

The district requires that I observe and document all content area literacy practices in all classrooms. Since I was unable to observe these in your class last week, I will be observing in your room again this Friday. Please send me your lesson plan, with your content area literacy activities highlighted, by 3:00 p.m. on Thursday.

Sincerely,

Dr. Anthony Nelson

The "solution": Before her observation on Friday, Anita meets with Anthony to explain the reasons for her approach and to highlight where her students are engaging in content area literacy practices. She begins by explaining how mathematical texts are different from the primarily print texts used in other disciplines. Anthony's teaching background is in social studies, so she knows he is thinking of text in a classical sense: words, sentences, paragraphs, and so on. In a mathematics class, Anita tells Anthony, students are reading and writing through different forms of text. Equations, symbols, graphs, drawings, and even physical manipulatives are considered text in mathematics. When Anita asks students to act out a problem or to use x as a variable in an equation, she is asking them to engage in literacy as they read the symbols and write equations. Anita explains that her goal is to have students engage in authentic literacy practices that make sense in a mathematics classroom.

In the lesson that Anthony observed, students were beginning an exploration of proportional reasoning, using a sampling capture-recapture activity. She tells him that because this was the first exploratory lesson on proportional reasoning, her students would not have been able to contribute anything to a KWL chart. They know little or nothing about proportional reasoning, to the degree that they don't even know enough about it to say what they want to know, which makes the "L" column unnecessary. Taking a literacy practice that is designed for a different content area such as language arts or social studies and simply inserting it into a math lesson for the sake of checking content area literacy off a mental checklist of things to do, she asserts, would involve a distortion of the purpose of both the instrument and the discipline of mathematics.

Anita ends her meeting with Anthony by showing him her lesson plan for the following day. In it, she has highlighted the following activities as mathematics literacy practices.

1. Students will use manipulatives to model a proportional reasoning problem.

2. Students will use a think-pair-share protocol to discuss their models and to introduce formal vocabulary in proportional reasoning.

3. Students will use tables to organize the data they collect in their exploration and will begin to develop the formal algorithms and symbolic representations used in proportional reasoning.

The rationale for the instruction: Anita has been teaching long enough to see many fads and buzzwords in education come and go. Ultimately, her goal is to make sure that she is teaching each and every student in her classroom using methods that make sense in a mathematics classroom. Not all literacy procedures make sense for her students. By sharing with the principal what she knows about being literate in mathematics, Anita is helping to expand his expectations of content area literacy practices.

Anita begins with expanding the definition of text so that an observer can recognize when students are reading and writing in mathematics class. It is impossible to see literacy practices in mathematics without this expanded definition. By having her students model and discuss problems, they are authoring and reading authentic texts in mathematics. Her discussion of appropriate literacy practices will, she hopes, encourage Anthony to reconsider his strict adherence to the "district approved" list of content area literacy practices to look for during observations.

Questions for Reflection

1. What has Anita foregrounded in her definition of content area literacy in mathematics?

2. To what extent has her instruction helped students to become mathematically literate?

3. How effectively has Anita planned so as to provide her students with an authentic literacy experience?

4. What effects does Anita's discussion have on her principal's ability to recognize and value different literacy practices in the content areas?

5. What is the likelihood that Anthony will redefine his view of literacy practices in future mathematics classes?

6. If you were evaluating Anita as an administrator, how would you assess her teaching?

7. What does Anthony overlook in deciding to evaluate in this way, and what problems might follow from his decision to assess mathematics literacy in this manner?

8. What does Anita overlook in deciding to teach this way, and what problems might follow from her decision to teach mathematics literacy in this manner?

REFERENCES

Borasi, R., Siegel, M., Fonzi, J., & Smith, C. F. (1998). Using transactional reading strategies to support sense-making and discussion in mathematics classrooms: An exploratory study. *Journal for Research in Mathematics Education, 29,* 275–305. doi:10.2307/749791

Huff, D. (1954). *How to lie with statistics.* London, UK: Gollancz.

Moje, E. B. (2008). Foregrounding the disciplines in secondary literacy teaching and learning: A call for change. *Journal of Adolescent & Adult Literacy, 52,* 96–107. doi:10.1598/JA

National Council of Teachers of Mathematics. (2000). *Principles and standards for school mathematics* (4th ed.). Reston, VA: Author.

Polya, G. (1945). *How to solve it: A new aspect of mathematical method* (2nd ed.). Princeton, NJ: Princeton University Press.

Rosenblatt, L. (1995). *Literature as exploration* (5th ed.). New York, NY: Modern Language Association of America.

Shuard, H., & Rothery, A. (Eds.). (1984). *Children reading mathematics.* London, UK: John Murray.

Smagorinsky, P. (2011). *Vygotsky and literacy research: A methodological framework.* Boston, MA: Sense.

Smagorinsky, P., Cook, L., & Reed, P. (2005). The construction of meaning and identity in the composition and reading of an architectural text. *Reading Research Quarterly, 40,* 70–88. Retrieved from http://www.petersmagorinsky.net/About/PDF/RRQ/RRQ2005.pdf

Wilson, A. A. (2011). A social semiotics framework for conceptualizing content area literacies. *Journal of Adolescent & Adult Literacy, 54*(6), 435–444. doi:10.1598/JAAL.54.6.5

5 The Visual Space of Literacy in Art Education

Karinna Riddett-Moore
and Richard Siegesmund

What does it mean to be literate in the visual arts? How does one read and write the visual? The *Oxford English Dictionary* traces the etymology of literacy to being learned, and, in turn, to being competent within a discipline. Therefore, one could speak of literacy in the visual arts while never engaging the reading or writing of linguistic signs. The visual is a realm of perception in all of its manifestations. Perception certainly involves how people gather and sort data through their eyes, for vision is a data-processing system, not a recording system. However, perception is more than sight. It also involves all of the senses: the moist, pliable feel of clay; the soft throbbing audial rhythms of a sewing machine; the luxuriant smell of oil paint as it oozes from a tube.

Viewing art as a discipline of making meaning through sense, one that is distinct from or perhaps even antagonistic to language, resonates with art educators. There is a strong tradition within K–12 education to frame the curriculum of art education in a raw expressive visuality that prides itself as being separate from the written and spoken word. This tradition goes back to art education curricula inspired by theories of the unconscious (Freud, 1930/1961) that see the role of art in school as allowing the child[1] to flower (Lowenfeld, 1947). For many years, the mantra in art education curriculum was to give the child the materials and get out of the way. The less said, the better.

For the most part, contemporary art education continues to privilege curricula that emphasize studio production. Kids make art; art decorates schools. In this conception, visual literacy does not mean learning as recognized by other subject areas; it is a form of doing. Such a view is grounded in Bruner's (1960) classic formulation that curriculum should look to a discipline's expert practitioners for a benchmark to students' classroom activities. Artists make art; therefore, in art class, students should make art (Wachowiak & Clements, 2001). That logic seems straightforward and obvious. We call this view *artistic education* as we expect students to make art. The learner's *expression* is the rationale for instruction. In addition, learners develop both access to and an *appreciation* for cultural norms. Through the cultural lens, expression and appreciation become the backbone of literacy in art.

There is a different way to frame visual literacy. Taking issue with expression and appreciation as the goals of artistic literacy, John Dewey (1934) offered an alternative curricular view privileging *perception* and *communication*. Through attention to fine-grained relationships of sensory qualities, students learn to communicate in a realm outside linguistic, mathematical, and even visual symbols. For Dewey, art opens new possibilities of thinking. The artist is not a special messenger with something to say. Art is simply a profoundly human nonsymbolic language. Dewey's distinctive learning goals form the core of what we refer to as visual literacy.

DEWEY'S VISION OF ART EDUCATION

Dewey (1934) observed that "recognition is perception arrested before it has a chance to develop freely" (p. 52). Our urge to apply symbolic classification to the objects in our visual and sensory array dampens or even closes entirely our interest in looking deeply at something. For example, let's say that a woman who is sitting in a chair suddenly feels a slight warm pressure against her leg. She reaches down and feels luxuriant fur against her hand, and her fingers begin to massage supple flesh. There is an audial purr of satisfaction. All of this sensory delight would likely lessen if she simply felt the pressure, recognized that a cat was in the room, and, once this recognition was obtained and the object labeled, moved on with her thoughts and did not participate in any further sensory encounters with the creature. Once she has the symbol, the sensory details may easily become unnecessary. Such details may even be an encumbrance for the rapid processing of information, even though the fullest appreciation of a moment combines a heady combination of unfolding perceptual sensory awareness and symbolic recognition.

Dewey advocated resistance to symbolic recognition's premature obstruction of sensory perception. He felt we learn more by lingering in the experience, rather than classifying it and moving on. In his view, the lessons of art are exercises in suspending closure and remaining highly attuned to the fine-grained distinctions in the relations of sensory qualities. Artists, architects, musicians, dancers, and poets consciously work in places of raw perception in order to suspend their audience's urge to recognize. Through those moments of suspension, recognition never quite settles into its previous categories. Recognition is reorganized. We see anew. That fresh sight allows us to say new things, to read new things, to perceive again (and again) in new ways. Dewey called this outcome of art—the outcome that, in his view, is most significant—the reorganization of space and time.

FROM PERCEPTION TO THE AESTHETICS OF CARE

Dewey also recognized that skills in perception and communication (part of the reorganization of space and time) lead to empathy: the recognition of *being-in-relationship* to another, an object, or groups and systems. To linger in the moment of perception of the cat is to fully embrace being-in-relationship with this animal. To extend this example further, let's return to the illustration of the woman and the cat. Care emerges when the woman acknowledges empathy and acts in ways that are mindful of how she exists in these personal associations. In this case, perhaps she picks up the cat and reaches for a toy that both she and the animal, together, can interact with. In short, the sensory awareness that springs from attention to being-in-relationship can give rise to states of play.

Nel Noddings (1995) has observed that educators have no problem thinking of care as a pedagogical trait: We care for our students, we foster a caring community of learners. Yet no academic discipline claims care—and developing the playful qualitative sensory awareness that leads to it—as a learning outcome of its discipline. However, Dewey claimed such qualitative moments of empathy and care as aesthetics. Thus, we argue, empathy and care are goals that belong to the discipline of visual art. To be visually literate requires demonstrations of empathy and care.

Empathy is an imaginative skill (Greene, 2001). Empathic imaginative thinking that is educationally significant restructures perception in order to see new ways of being-in-relationship. We are in relationship with ourselves, the objects we touch, and those around us. The philosopher Michel Foucault (1988) suggested that through imaginative engagement we participate in the aesthetic task of rebuilding ourselves—an auto-deconstructive process through which we strive to new possibility. This view resonates with the ideas of Richard Rorty (1989), who contended that a principal aim of education is to create individuals who are *strong poets:* individuals who are capable of rewriting themselves repeatedly. Two core purposes of education are, first, to enable individuals to visualize new possible futures toward which they can aspire, and second, to set forth a pathway through which the individual can remake himself or herself for that future (Eisner, 2002). The act of rewriting moves through three steps:

1. To rewrite the self begins in visual perception. To see new possibilities requires attention to fine-grained qualities and sensory relationships to which one has previously not attended.

2. Acts of rewriting foster communication. We first inscribe meaning in the hope that we might learn through our experiences. Inscription also allows us to share our experiences with others.

3. In our learning to rewrite, we demonstrate care. Our first acts of rewriting are demonstrations of the care-of-self, attempts to declare that our experiences have private, personal value. However, these inscriptions lead to the care-of-others as we share our own attempts at inscription and recognize the courage of others' life stories. Foucault (1988) claimed that engagement with these two acts of care produced an *arts of living*, a perfection of the self that leads to an ethical perfection of society. Thus, we argue that in visual art, care is more than a pedagogical affect; it is an effect of learning: Caring is an educational outcome. Therefore, literacy in the visual arts requires demonstrations by the student of awareness of being-in-relation. Literacy in the visual arts is the ability to engage, through a rewriting of self, with an arts of living, based on perception and acts of care.

THE CHALLENGES AND POSSIBILITIES OF VISUAL LITERACY

The visual arts are both blessed and cursed in the K–12 curriculum because they are not treated as a serious area of study. There are, indeed, voluntary national standards for the visual arts as well as standards written by every state for teaching art. However, what is missing is mandatory testing. Even if government agencies have dutifully written standards for the arts and made solemn pronouncements that the arts are core, schools are held accountable only to government-required tests. What is tested is taught. Consequently, the arts often find themselves marginalized within—and at worst, cut from—the curriculum.

The lack of external sanctioned tests pressures art teachers to produce their own standards of assessment, and this need often pushes them to emphasize skills training. Scoring artistic technique is straightforward, in much the same way that a connoisseur scores a figure skater's performance of a double axel jump—a maneuver that delights the general viewer—through the analysis of a precise sequence of categories. Not only is it possible to create rubrics for the assessment of skills, but scorers can also construct assessments for the expression of meaning.

Unfortunately, these assessments are frequently as banal as asking students to explain the significance of the green light at the end of the dock in *The Great Gatsby,* for such reflections are readily downloaded from the Internet. Students are just as cynical about the "meaning game" in visual arts as they are in language arts. Such tests only meet a hermetic "school art" criterion (Efland, 1976): standards that work within the culture and expectations of K–12 school, but have little relevance outside this context. In contrast, we view visual literacy as a skill that prepares students to navigate the world outside school.

SCENARIOS

The following scenarios make the case for rejecting the art-for-art's sake paradigm for what it means to be learned in the visual. While there is content in the visual arts—bricks of knowledge—the acquisition of core knowledge, and agility with handling these bricks, should not be confused with what it means to be literate, especially if an aspect of visual literacy requires demonstration of being in empathetic relationships.

When we allow students to delve into richly melded curricular pools, not confining them to the content of a discreet discipline, they can thrive. Consequently, visual literacy should not be taught as a stand-alone skill, defined within the confines of a fifty-minute class period and discrete unto itself. Rather, visual literacy opens the door to deeply integrative literacy practices. It is essential for students to engage in integrative literacies so that they may become visually literate.

SCENARIO 1: The *Pietà* Is a Love Letter

The setting: St. Michael's is an independent parochial middle school in a suburban area outside a major city. The area hosts one of the largest public school districts and many established, renowned independent schools. The school serves Grades 1 through 8 with about 76 percent of the population European American and mostly middle to upper class, 10 percent African American, 8 percent Asian American, and 6 percent Latino/a students. About 8 percent of the population receives tuition scholarships or a reduction in tuition.

The characters: This scenario includes eighteen students in the eighth grade, ages fourteen or fifteen. All will be attending an educational international trip to Rome during the spring semester. The school's art instructor, Elizabeth Hesse, will be serving as head chaperone for this trip.

The context: Elizabeth is given the task of writing an art history curriculum that will prepare these students to experience the art of Rome and the Vatican. The following are some factors that contribute to the curriculum and instruction.

- The middle school curriculum is college preparatory, an orientation that produces standards of excellence in standardized testing designed to rank the school among the highest in the state. Students have a rigorous core academic schedule, taking Language Arts, World History, Life and Earth Science, Algebra 1, Spanish, and Religion in a block schedule format, allowing for eighty-minute periods in all core classes, which meet roughly three times a week. Electives (the visual arts, music, and physical education) are also on a block schedule, but they run for one-hour periods twice a week. Because of this schedule, and partially because of the expectations of parents for students to succeed in all academic areas, students often view their art and music classes as the bottom rungs of the ladder, electing to skip any homework assignments in favor of the classes that "count."
- Elizabeth works within a framework of her state Visual Arts Performance Standards that emphasize teaching art as an ethics of care and responsibility.[2]
- From her experience working with middle school students, Elizabeth understands that her students must be invested in their learning experiences in the arts in order for the arts to have an impact on their daily lives. She strives to teach them in a way that is relational, experiential, and meaningful. While the facts about the artwork and history of Rome are important, she realizes that authentic engagement will come from exploring the themes in the work on a personal level first, rather than on a strictly factual level.
- The private school setting affords a flexible curriculum. However, parents are highly involved in their children's education and performance. They want to know they are getting their money's worth in education. In other schools like St. Michael's, parents' perception of what is being taught, or what should be taught, often influences the administration and, likewise, the teachers.

The dilemma: Not all students at St. Michael's are Catholic or Christian. Elizabeth's teaching experience began in a public school setting, so she is sensitive to the needs of all her students. She believes that the academic emphasis on the artwork of the Vatican should engage all students regardless of their faith or religious beliefs. However, she does not want to limit content to the formal elements and principles of design in the artwork. She wants to emphasize what is common to humanity, rather than Christianity, while still working within the expectations of a predominantly Christian school community. Elizabeth is engaged in an ongoing dilemma in art education: how to appropriately address issues of faith and culture within a work of art without ignoring or de-emphasizing the religious context. She is also faced with creating a curriculum that meets the expectations of an administration that strongly supports content knowledge and traditional learning environments, yet still affords the flexible, individualized outcomes that arise from engaging students in a curriculum designed to develop an "arts of living." In other words, she is struggling to determine how she can teach being-in-relation with religious works of art in a way that can prompt all students to begin to develop their own ethic of care and that can deepen the students' understanding of themes present in the works of art studied.

The "solution": Elizabeth decides to teach a lesson on Michelangelo's *Pietà*, the Renaissance marble masterpiece that depicts Mary holding the body of Jesus on her lap following the Crucifixion. The theme she emphasizes is *love*. Instead of beginning the art history lesson with the work of art, she begins with students' perceptions and understandings of love. There are four segments to this lesson, briefly summarized here.

1. Critical analysis of a love song. Each student chooses an appropriate love song, any song that exemplifies a definition of love or a love story, yet contains no profanity. The students then take turns listening to the love songs within a small group of three or four, and write a paragraph-long critical analysis.[3] The analysis must list the songwriter's definition of love; the style (genre) and mood of the song; any symbols, similes, or metaphors; and a personal statement giving the students' perception and agreement on the artist/songwriter's message or definition of love.

2. Visual representation of the selected love song. After the groups share their definitions of love, Elizabeth makes a class list, dividing the topics into visual imagery and definitions of love. She then guides students through an exercise in creating visual representations of the parts of one love song, which she has chosen herself. She provides this model in order to demonstrate what she expects of them when they create their final work of art using their song of choice. In this exercise, the class discusses how visual elements, such as color, can communicate the mood of a song. A sad love song might have muted colors, or use a cool color family, while an upbeat club song might employ bright, analogous colors to convey excitement and energy. Students are also encouraged in this part of the assignment to enhance their drawing skills, using objects from real life to assist them in drawing the imagery or symbols present in the song.

This segment of the lesson concerns the production of art, with each student taking a personal interpretive direction. However, Elizabeth strategically pulls in artists whose work might influence the direction the students have chosen to take. For example, one student is interested in using only color and simple lines and shapes to portray his song, so Elizabeth shares the work of color field and abstract expressionist artists who tackle the same concept. For students who enjoy drawing the parts of their song literally, using figures or realistic drawing, Elizabeth shares appropriate paintings of artists such as Gustav Klimt, Mary Cassatt, or Jacob Lawrence. Criteria for this segment include displaying an understanding of color relationships, symbolic imagery, layering, cultural influences, and overall unity in composition.

3. Multimedia viewing of the *Pieta*. Students then imagine they have been taken prisoner with someone they love, whom they must describe by traits alone (e.g., someone who has seen them cry, someone who has always been there for them, someone who loves them for who they are, and other shared intimate occasions or dispositions). The reflection ends in the imagined loved one dying to save the student. Students then view a slideshow of Michelangelo's *Pietà,* with multiple images of the sculpture set to a love song, "If You Want Me To," by Ginny Owens. Students are also given short segments of text to read about the sculpture for homework.

4. Personal reflection or love letter as summative assessment. The final class period of this lesson is devoted to two activities: a critique of the final works of art based on the love songs, and a written reflection about love. Students may choose one of the following journal prompts and answer with written words only, or with words and images together.

- **Prompt 1:** How does Michelangelo's *Pietà* express love between a mother and son? Give at least three visual elements (such as line, color, form, space, or texture) to support your statements. Define the love that this sculpture portrays, as you see it. Use some imagery or symbolism that you found present in the love songs we shared in class.
- **Prompt 2:** Write a love letter from the perspective of one of the figures in the sculpture. Write it as if they were speaking it now, as they are frozen in this pose. Include at least three visual elements in the letter. Consider the moment they are both caught in (e.g., between life and death, hope and despair). Consider your own reflection from the imaginative reflection about being taken prisoner with a loved one. How does it feel to have someone die for you?

With each of these segments, Elizabeth assigns assessable criteria that emphasize the learning outcomes yet require a personal response from the students. By assigning the criteria of naming visual elements, the academic language of visual art, to support students' analysis, Elizabeth is able to assess their ability to decipher visual qualities and relate empathetically to those qualities. The assignment doesn't simply ask for students' opinions about the work of art, but rather asks for students to tap into their perception of the piece and how they relate to the universal meanings behind the work of art.

Student Example

The way I see it, Michelangelo's *Pietà* is a love letter. The female figure that represents Mary holds her son, Jesus, who is dead. Her face is not in agony though; not strained. It is peaceful and sad. As if she is saying, "Goodbye for now," like a mother would who is just putting her son to bed. Her left hand extends out, open, not supporting his body. It is as if she is giving him up to God. Her love is his support. Love here is like the stone. It is stable and supporting. It is also smooth, soft, and flows like the fabric. There are two figures, but one love, one stone. The love is pure and white. It reminds me of a love that is eternal.

The rationale for the instruction: Each segment of this lesson contains literacy goals within the framework of visual arts. Art education, as conceived here, focuses on relating to artwork as a way to communicate and attempts to close the gap between makers of art and viewers of art. Students can enter into a space of relationship with a work of art from their own perspective, with their own questions, thoughts, and values. This lesson is meant to affect their experiences in art and within the art world. Art history is not a topic to master (content knowledge), but rather a lesson in experience and relationship. When Elizabeth asks students to create their own visual interpretations of a love song, she is valuing their ideas about love and their ability to express those ideas visually. She is also encouraging them to relate to the mind of an artist, not just to the finished outcome of the work of art.

When learners study the history of art, they do not just view objects; they relate to them. Learning how to relate to works of art means approaching a work from a deeply personal, experiential level. The question of content changes significantly. Instead of asking the students, "What do you know about Michelangelo?" Elizabeth is asking them, "What do you know about love? Where does your definition of love come from? How do you express love to others? How has love been expressed historically and/or religiously through art?" Such a lesson benchmarks the outcome of an art education based on developing an "art of living." These activities can help students learn to care and develop as ethical beings.

Questions for Reflection

1. How has Elizabeth defined visual literacy within this lesson?

2. If this lesson were used in a public school classroom, would the *Pietà* be an appropriate subject on which to build the activities, or might the lesson require adaptation using secular art? If adaptation is necessary, how might you adjust the lesson for your public school students?

3. How might this lesson encourage students to become strong poets, or individuals who are able to rewrite themselves?

4. What writing/thinking/relationship skills does this lesson help develop?

5. How might students be assessed in their ability to communicate through visual expression?

6. How do you view instruction of this sort in light of recent demands for school accountability via standardized tests?

7. In what ways could ideas from Elizabeth's class be applied across the school curriculum?

8. To what degree is this approach compatible with national standards mandates, and how might you modify the activities to fit within requirements you might face in meeting the school's mission to be highly ranked according to test scores?

9. How might Elizabeth fare on existing teacher evaluation instruments that rate her effectiveness and determine her merit?

10. If existing evaluation instruments are not sensitive to what she accomplishes, what sort of alternative would you propose to provide a more valid means of measuring her effectiveness?

SCENARIO 2: *PostSecret:* Finding Narrative in Image and Text[4]

The setting: Shadyside High School serves approximately 1,400 students and is located on the fringe of a metropolitan area. Its demographics closely mirror the region as a whole, with a student population that is 60 percent European American and 35 percent African American. Latino/a, Asian American, and Native American populations make up the rest. Thirty-five percent of the student population is eligible for free or reduced-price lunch. There is a stark economic divide between segments of the European American and African American student populations. A number of the European American Shadyside students come from surrounding neighborhoods that serve as exurbs to a major city thirty miles to the east. These students come from corporate-oriented families, whereas other Shadyside students come from neighborhoods where the dynamics of agriculture prevail. Politically, the district splits along racial lines. However, both communities are deeply religious and socially conservative. Students—particularly those from impoverished backgrounds—arrive facing a host of academic challenges, but by senior year, 96 percent of the students pass the state exit exam on their first attempt.

The characters: Lisa Jaeger is one of two art instructors at Shadyside. She has a master's of education degree, which also involved a teaching assistantship through the Writing Intensive Program (WIP) of the university's Department of Literacy Education. In her graduate work, Lisa worked with preservice art education students to develop curriculum that would engage students in writing through art production.

Now in her second year of teaching art, Lisa teaches an Art 1 class to thirty-two students at Shadyside. The class comprises a broad range of learners, including students from all four years, athletes, students with special needs, African American students from blue-collar families, students from highly agrarian backgrounds, and students whose families are profoundly corporate in orientation. A few of the students actually want to study art, but many are looking for some easy credits and a respite from the grueling work of school in general.

The context: Because of her WIP instruction, Lisa recognizes that writing is an iterative process—that is, one that involves cycles of a sequence of processes. She recognizes potential connections between communicating with words and communicating with images. With language, she works to incorporate multiple informal (low stakes) forms of writing to capture quick ideas—writing to sketch—through which a student can test an idea. For example, the student's personal visual journals provide a permanent, assessable record of image and linguistic ideation. Later, students can refine these spontaneous forms of writing into high-stakes writing. She uses the same process to help her students develop visual images: sketch and refine. The same process works with both words and images. This cycle forms the heart of her curriculum.

The factors influencing Lisa's instruction include the following:

- *Support from her colleague, who has a bachelor's degree from the same university, and from her principal, who has been captivated by her view of how to teach literacy since her initial interview for her position at Shadyside.* In particular, the principal is impressed by her ability to articulate outcomes—how students will authentically engage with language. Lisa is a visual arts specialist, and yet at the same time she has received graduate training in writing pedagogy from her university's Department of Literacy Education. Her training has not been limited to one academic discipline; she has a deeply integrative perspective on teaching and learning. As a new teacher at Shadyside, she received regular visits to her classroom from her administration. She took advantage of these moments when she had the administration's attention to quickly review her curriculum goals. She made an effort to share her thinking with her superiors. She took the initiative to be sure that her supervisors knew what she was doing, as she knew her curriculum was innovative.
- *The absence of a state-mandated art test.* Although Lisa's approach seems slightly unorthodox, especially to those concerned with aligning the school's visual art curriculum with the state standards, the state has no art test to enforce its standards of learning, so Lisa is unencumbered by this problem.
- *Students' ability to use both the language of the visual and the linguistic to communicate.* Lisa understands that images do more than illustrate words, and she wants to challenge her students to think about how visual materials might tell more than words can say.

The following lesson outline gives an example of this type of curriculum.

PostSecret *Project Summary*

1. Lisa's lessons build on a template of low-stakes integrated image making and writing followed by more polished and sophisticated work. She bases one of her low-stakes lessons on Frank Warren's *PostSecret.* Warren started *PostSecret* in 2004 by randomly distributing blank self-addressed postcards to strangers throughout the Washington, DC, area. With the cards, he provided instructions that invited the recipient to share a true, but never previously revealed, secret. He asked the writers

to remain anonymous and to be creative. He made no specific demand that imagery be included—only that the writing be brief and legible. However, people spontaneously chose to combine images and words when asked to communicate concisely. The cards that came back to Warren were beautiful.[5] Lisa gives students blank postcards and asks them to follow the same directions, turning the postcards in to her anonymously.

2. The *PostSecret* framework is the epitome of low-stakes writing and image making because there are so few requirements. Students may submit more than one secret, and there never is a problem with participation. There are always plenty of cards dropped off into the class collection box. When the first round of writing and image making is complete, the class views students' cards. Some are silly or adolescently provocative (e.g., "I'm in love with my art teacher"), yet some hint at more somber secrets, perhaps including depression, child abuse, and the trauma of an abortion. Students' work embraces the concepts of revelation and confession, providing the safe place for students to be as they are. Some of these cards may serve as alerts so that Lisa can initiate appropriate levels of help and support, but the primary educational purpose is not diagnostic. She seeks to create a place of emotional centeredness from which each student can begin art making. This emotional emphasis also creates an environment of caring, which is consistent with teaching an arts of living beyond the individual and into the community of the classroom.

3. As the art teacher, Lisa steers the students' discussion toward how individual cards demonstrate the use of visual imagery to support language. She points to a card with washed-out, bleeding colors that speak to the author's purported struggle with depression. She asks the students to consider how the dissipated green, grayed with a touch of red, conveys the feeling of what it is to be depressed: how, in Dewey's (1934) terms, the media draws forth the meaning of the word.

4. As the unit continues, the low stakes of *PostSecret* move into more sophisticated visual objects that combine increasingly elaborated narrative writing and image making. These later works are the portfolio pieces: the works that students will submit for competitions and awards. Nevertheless, the *PostSecret* lesson opens the door to a range of activities. It is a critical place of beginning.

5. At the year-end school open house, Lisa decides to devote a section of her presentation wall, outside her classroom, to the *PostSecret* cards. She is well aware that some of what has been shared behind the closed classroom wall cannot go into the public space of the school hallway, so she judiciously edits some of the more provocative responses out of the public display.

The dilemma: At the open house, one of Shadyside's high-striving parents is outraged by the *PostSecret* section of the art exhibit and confronts Lisa. The parent makes a scene, in front of other parents and students, claiming that the work is not art and that the content is scandalous and disrespectful. Furthermore, the cards do not suggest that Lisa is *teaching*. She is not in control of the outcomes of her class. She insists that Lisa take the cards down immediately. Lisa, as a skilled yet still novice teacher, attempts to keep her composure and explains the curricular justification for the work. As a former competitive athlete of considerable achievement, she knows how to remain calm under pressure. The incensed parent tells Lisa that she will report her to the principal and advocate for her removal from her position. Lisa manages to holds back her tears until she gets home.

The "solution": Following the incident at the open house, Lisa takes the initiative. She does not wait for the principal to come to her; she goes to the principal, who supports her. He recognizes the arc of her curriculum and sees the learning objectives, the ends she holds in view. He notes that these are so much more than what he has previously expected from his visual arts specialists, and he concludes that Lisa has exceeded his expectations toward contributing to the overall curricular goals of the school. They decide that her curriculum has worked for the students, and he offers to deal with the concerned parent.

The rationale for the instruction: Lisa's visual art process is deeply informed by Louise Rosenblatt's reader response theory (2005), which states that literacy is the meaning that the reader makes from a text, not the reader's ability to correctly interpret the "official" meaning of the text. Students' meanings are messy, and this interpretive reality is what shocked the parent who confronted Lisa at the open house. The parent viewed these personal meanings as evidence that Lisa was not properly managing her classroom, which, in the parent's view, meant steering students to the "right" answer.

Lisa's curriculum, both the visual and literary, is also shaped by Donald Murray's (1996) concept of the writing process. *PostSecret* is a form of prewriting. It is a place of gathering one's thoughts. The collective sharing of work is also a form of prewriting, because students are exposed to the potential of what they might consider and act upon. Their engagement with additional dimensions of a composing process—drafting ideas, reflecting and revising, getting feedback, fine-tuning, and sharing—moves their thinking and their compositions from raw experience to representation of experience to textual form that others can in turn interpret through the lens of their own understandings.

Questions for Reflection

1. Lisa has to deal with a class where many of the students, if not most, do not want to study her discipline. She cannot fall back on attempting to intimidate her students into learning by saying, "You have to know this for the test if you want to graduate," as there is no high-stakes testing in visual arts. What is her strategy for engaging the class in wanting to learn?

2. Lisa attempts to meld the drawing process and writing process into a single unified curriculum. Although trained by her university's Department of Literacy Education

in how to teach the writing process, Lisa is not a certified Language Arts teacher. Her school has a Language Arts curriculum separate from what she is doing. Is she out of bounds? Is this inappropriate instruction? What if a Language Arts teacher began teaching students to draw in her class? Is this appropriate?

3. Historically, art has served to provoke, shock, disturb, and otherwise upset conventional thinking. Do teachers have a responsibility to cultivate this value, or should they impose limits on what students may express through their art? If students represent harmful actions through their art, does the art teacher have a responsibility to intervene with the school's counseling and legal personnel?

4. Lisa's ability to weather the parental complaint relied on her ability to articulate learning objectives in her classroom that exceeded state standards. What was she asking her students to do? How does this compare with the Language Arts standards of your state?

5. Lisa's university's College of Education's Language Arts certification program, not the Department of English, trained her in teaching the writing process. Because of this training, is there a difference in the attitude that she brought to her curriculum?

6. If English teachers had more training in art, would their teaching of writing be different? If so, how? If not, why not?

7. In what ways can ideas from Lisa's class be applied across the school curriculum?

8. To what degree is this approach compatible with national standards mandates, and how might you modify the activities to fit within requirements you might face in meeting the school's mission to be highly ranked according to test scores?

9. How might Lisa fare on existing teacher evaluation instruments that rate her effectiveness and determine her merit?

10. If existing evaluation instruments are not sensitive to what she accomplishes, what sort of alternative would you propose to provide a more valid means of measuring her effectiveness?

SCENARIO 3: Doodles Can Mean Something

The setting: Fiskar Ridge Preparatory School is a middle-to-upper-grade public charter school just inside the perimeter of a mid-eastern city. While it is not directly a part of the public city schools, it is home to a diverse population of sixth through twelfth graders, many of whom live several miles outside the city. It has recently earned International Baccalaureate (IB) Accreditation for its Middle Years Programme (MYP). The student population is fairly balanced, with about 30 percent European American, 25 percent Asian American, 20 percent African American, and 25 percent Latino/a. Most of these students are new to the IB curriculum[6] and approach to learning.

The characters: James Blick teaches Drawing & Painting to a variety of students in Grades 6 through 8 as a mixed-level and mixed-age class. Students have partial decision making in what art class they elect to take, but they are all required to take at least one art class during the year. The class enrolls twenty-eight students, all with different levels of art instruction and with various degrees of competency in the arts.

The context:

- Because of the school's charter and IB status, students are enrolling at Fiskar Ridge Prep at a high rate. While this interest brings a diverse population, it also brings large discrepancies of academic preparation. Some have had art instruction in elementary school, and some have not.

- In the MYP of the IB curriculum, literacy in the arts is traditionally seen as artistic education (see this chapter's introduction), or the mastery of artistic skills that mimic cultural forms. However, IB does recognize the value in nonverbal ways of communicating and promotes international understanding throughout all areas of study. The philosophy that guides the MYP is concerned with the concepts of intercultural awareness, holistic learning, and communication. Service learning and community interaction are also stressed throughout the curriculum.

- James now has the task of developing an art curriculum that meets the expectations of art making within the IB framework, as well as addressing the wide variety of abilities of his students. He is also asked by his principal to incorporate some aspect of service learning into this curriculum and pedagogy, as IB teachers are encouraged to model learning and service as well as teach about it.

- At the beginning of the semester, a devastating earthquake strikes Haiti. Fiskar Ridge Prep immediately begins a fundraiser to support a local doctor (also a parent at the school) who leads a relief mission trip to attend to the people of Haiti. An overwhelming response from the community funds the medical trip within days of the announcement.

- Despite the laudable financial support for the relief efforts, James notices that the students of his Drawing & Painting class do not grasp the magnitude of the event or the poverty of the Haitian people, or the role of the United States in contributing to Haitian poverty (Angulo, 2012). The middle and early high school students seem to be empathetically unaware of their connection to the citizens of Haiti. Although the community has donated money and medical supplies, the students themselves appear to lack the felt connection to giving that authentic charity requires. It is more likely that the students themselves did not experience an act of charity, but rather relayed one from their families. The students seem to have missed the educational lesson of increased intercultural awareness and empathy. The citizens of Haiti are distant sufferers to them, people with whom they have little in common. James chooses to addresses the issue of suffering as the next project in the Drawing & Painting class. He asks students to design a work of art that might help other teens in their school empathize with the citizens of Haiti. In the form of IB learning, he lets the students research the events happening in Haiti, ranging from the relief efforts to the living conditions after the earthquake.

The dilemma: The students share their ideas in class, and the response is strong. They have elaborate visions of life-sized murals depicting a Haitian teenager's life alongside a comfortable American teen's life. Many other ideas mirror this one, such as landscapes of broken buildings with silhouettes of Haitian families. James is conscientious in helping students understand that caring for others in need should not also serve to pathologize them. This empathic dimension of care is often not shared toward people from societies whose standard of living is based on values other than those that guide life in the United States. Rather than emphasizing the Haitians' poverty as a societal deficiency, he hopes to help students understand the conditions that produce their abject circumstances, and empathize with their plight of living in wreckage without immediate relief in terms of food, water, shelter, and medical care, and without long-term resources for rebuilding a sturdier infrastructure and building structures.

One problem arises with each idea: The students cannot (and frequently resist) drawing figures, claiming that figures are just too hard. James senses the hesitancy of the students, and knows he cannot teach them acceptable figure drawing in the amount of time allotted for this lesson. The message of the artwork will be lost because of the students' varied abilities and skills. His job, however, is to develop their skills while encouraging them to retain these thematic issues in their art. In a short period of time, students need basic skills training, but this instruction will be empty if the deeper meaning of empathetic care is lost. To teach these dimensions of care, James needs to plan activities that will allow students to think on five levels of care. Specifically, students will need to do the following:

1. Consider how they are in relationship to objects they come in contact with and manipulate.

2. Begin to appreciate how these relationships with objects begin to define who they are—or whom they wish to be.

3. Share these personal understandings with peers in their class and recognize how their peers are dealing with these forms of being-in-relationship.

4. Project how, as a class, they exist in the school.

5. Make the final step and understand how they are in-relationship with the people of Haiti.

The "solution": James recognizes that students' perception often begins in simply noting what they can see. In his personal art library, James finds a visual sketching and journal activity that deals with consumption—that is, the purchasing and usage behaviors of people in society. The activity requires minimal skills. The task merely asks students to record, in image and word, everything they consume in a day, from sheets of toilet paper to the estimated amount of water both drunk and used for cleaning, tending to plants, and other deployments. This activity requires students to slow down, pay attention, and notice their surroundings. It is an exercise in reflection and aesthetic lingering. It will give value to the everyday objects of James's students. Yet, the students have to experience purposeful lingering.

James assigns the activity as a sketchbook exercise and requires the students to draw and write all they consume over a three-day period. He introduces this lesson to the class by providing a few examples of how to create simple sketches of everyday objects, and by turning the drawing lesson into an exercise on contour line and value, size relationships, and other standard art concepts.

When the students return from the activity, they reflect on what they learned. They write about their sketches and compare them with what they learned from researching about the relief efforts in Haiti. The activity "clicks" for some of the students, and they make statements such as the following: "We have so much, and they have so little. We need to show that. 'Cause it's all this daily stuff we have, iPods and things like my bagel, and I threw half of it away. That's what we have to show the other kids here with our art." They decide to create life-sized silhouettes of themselves and fill their silhouettes with the consumption doodles. They trace one life-sized image of a Haitian teenager taken from a photograph and fill it with the ration of water, rice, and medical supplies this teen might receive in a day. Tracing bypasses the skills-acquisition problem of learning how to render a human figure by hand. The final work of art is simple—pencil drawings piled inside of butcher paper silhouettes. Ten complete silhouettes hang in the hallway opposite one silhouette of the Haitian teenager.

In the final critique of the project, the students share something they have learned, what they might change, or what they consider the strongest part of their work. One student, who has a reputation for being the artist in her grade level because of her ability to draw realistically, says, "I learned how to doodle with this project. I don't doodle 'cause I want everything to be finished and complete, like shaded and stuff." When James asks what was different about the doodles in her sketchbook and her final piece, she answers, "The doodle means something more like that [points to everyone's portraits together]. The ones in my sketchbook are just what *I* did, what *I* ate or whatever. But when you see them all together, and just in *everyone*'s sketch style—like handwriting—the doodle means something."

The rationale for the instruction: Two major shifts in art pedagogy and visual literacy are evident in this scenario. First, a student changes her view about the definition of art through the exercise of doodling. In her world, she has always defined valid drawing as realistic drawing, which produces successful products whose composition is predetermined, wins her praise and admiration, and earns her the label (and identity) of class artist. Yet now she is willing to admit that this new way of drawing (for her), the doodle, has its place in conveying meaning, perhaps even in a more powerful way than realistic portraits might do. In this moment of admission, she opens herself to the value of the preliminary composing that writing teachers call *prewriting*. She recognizes that there is something raw and natural, fresh and alive about the repetition of the doodle in these portraits. Simple drawings of napkins, toothpaste, crackers, soap, toast, gum, water bottles, and even electricity (usually in the form of lightning bolts or power cords) can serve as captivating and reflective works of art. The student makes, and conveys, meaning through a doodle.

This transformation becomes available when James alters his sketchbook assignments from tasks in realistic depiction to exercises driven by meaning. He creates an art environment based on the *theme* of consumption, rather than the raw skills of life drawing. In other words, he shifts from *artistic technique* to *meaning* in art. Consumption is a big idea, a part of students' life-world. It is a theme that crosses curricular boundaries and glides into every part of their education, yet is rarely discussed with educational rigor. By making meaningful expression the center point of the lesson, James points to the value of art in sharing what is personal and meaningful within the context of community, rather than outside it. It allows his curriculum to shift from rendering a visual object to the expression of meaningful ideas.

The second shift in visual literacy changes the focus to aesthetics as a philosophy of care and responsible choice. James focuses on students' development of an ethical and empathetic worldview through drawing. By valuing their ideas and leveling the playing field of students' technical abilities by focusing on the readily accessible skill of "doodling," he communicates to the students that to be literate in the visual arts is to relate to others through art making. There is something to be valued in the aimless marks made on the edges of paper or in the margins of history notes. Students get the message that if art is to be a part of their daily lives, it must not be severed from them. This theme guides the message of Dewey's writing. Visual literacy is learning the tools of the arts in order to relate to, and care for, the other. In this case, a doodle becomes a tool for helping students grasp the abstract and connect to those people whose needs they can help relieve.

Questions for Reflection

1. The students in James's class donated money and brought in medical supplies to support the Haitian relief efforts. This charity is admirable. Why would James see this activity as a literacy problem with his students?

2. How does slowing down to notice form provide a critical prelude that allows students to achieve a more sophisticated layer of understanding about how they are in relationship to people in Haiti?

3. Much of what is expected in corporate approaches to education emphasizes productivity and information. What values from an arts education approach predicated on slowing down to appreciate meaning and imagine how to represent it

are of value in other areas of the corporate-influenced curriculum? If the two are at odds, how might they be reconciled instructionally?

4. Discuss the five levels of care that James wants his students to engage in this lesson. How do the students demonstrate—in observable, assessable ways—these levels of care? How do these levels demonstrate literacy?

5. How does group work become a critical part of literacy in this lesson?

6. In what ways can ideas from James's class be applied across the school curriculum?

7. Art can be controversial, and U.S. schools tend to depict America unproblematically as an "exceptional" place and a force for moral good in world progress (Loewen, 1996). If a student's research into Haiti found that, according to some, American business interests have helped to produce Haiti's poverty (e.g., Goel, 2011), should the teacher allow such a perspective to be expressed through art, or discourage it?

8. To what degree is this approach compatible with national standards mandates, and how might you modify the activities to fit within requirements you might face in meeting the school's mission to be highly ranked according to test scores?

9. How might James fare on existing teacher evaluation instruments that rate his effectiveness and determine his merit?

10. If existing evaluation instruments are not sensitive to what he accomplishes, what sort of alternative would you propose to provide a more valid means of measuring his effectiveness?

SCENARIO 4: Shifting Control: Teaching White Girl to Dance

The setting: Gateway Middle School is in an ostensibly rural area, but it exhibits many of the same challenges of poverty that face urban schools. The school has close to six hundred students, evenly divided among the sixth, seventh, and eighth grades. Demographically, the school is more than 50 percent African American, 30 percent European American, 10 percent Latino/a, and 10 percent Asian American. Seventy percent of the student population is eligible for free or reduced-price lunch. The educational disparities in these groups are in evidence on the mandatory state academic assessment exam. A quarter of the African American and Latino/a students, many of whom live under difficult economic circumstances, do not meet Language Arts grade-level standards, as measured by standardized tests. Fewer than 5 percent of European American students, meanwhile, perform beneath the standards. Longitudinal testing shows that these performance levels remain stable over the three years that students remain at Gateway. Out of each graduating class of two hundred students, then, the test scores of about one out of every six students will not improve appreciably.

The characters: Amanda Williams, the art specialist, holds dual certification in Art and Language Arts. She has been teaching at Gateway Middle school for the entire six years of her career to date. Her teacher preparation in art was "old school": Give the kids the materials and get out of the way. However, the realities of her students' lives have made her seriously question that approach. She recognizes that letting kids make cool stuff does not help them to critically re-imagine their lives and that imagining the possibility of another way of living is essential for their futures. Without this chance, she believes, they may easily be limited to a cycle of poverty.

Amanda has come to the realization that her students do not need therapeutic busywork with their hands that might keep them occupied and out of trouble. This approach does not advance their academic learning or personal development. Rather, they need to envision a way to reinvent themselves as a way to provide themselves with more options in life. She has begun to change the way she teaches accordingly.

Overall, the faculty regards Amanda as a leader. Her administration and peers recognize that something happens to the students who enter Amanda's art room. They are transformed. No one can quite explain what it is that she is doing, but everyone acknowledges the results.

The context: With so many students performing below grade level, many teachers in the school experience classroom management challenges in teaching the curriculum, which is pitched to skill levels and understandings outside these students' range of experience. These teachers complain that struggling students often disrupt their classrooms, even though the principal has manipulated enrollments to distribute them across the classroom assignments in order to put them in the company of higher-performing students, who presumably model more acceptable school conduct and elevate academic expectations for them.

Most of these kids are tough, and many solve problems through violence as a means of ensuring their status within their subculture. There are emergency buzzers in the classrooms of Gateway for use if violence erupts in a classroom.

Meeting Adequate Yearly Progress benchmarks—always a struggle for Gateway Middle—has particularly challenged the faculty for the last two years, and many blame the students themselves for performances that imply that they are ineffective teachers. There is pressure on everyone to try to help those students who show the most promise of responding to instruction, such that they serve as the "tide that lifts all boats" in elevating test scores. The lower-achieving students are viewed, meanwhile, as weights that pull the boats down and prohibit advances in measures of achievement.

Amanda, however, views these low-performing students as having personal and academic potential, and she focuses her efforts on their learning and individual growth through education. Specifically, she has requested that fourteen of the below-level eighth-grade students be pulled from their regular Language Arts classroom and given to her for a special block period class. She hopes to use visual art as a means to help these students engage fruitfully with the curriculum.

The dilemma: Amanda believes that all students can learn at high levels. However, she recognizes that numerous contextual factors can create a culture in which students choose not to learn because they intuitively perceive learning and behavioral conformity as forms of colonial domination. Furthermore, many find that resistance to school is a way to forge an identity among their peers. As an art teacher, Amanda believes that the appeal of visual media—the sensuous exploration of clay, the exhilaration of working with viscous paint, the calligraphic gestures in tagging, and other sensory means of engagement—are all means to lure resistant students to learning. However, much to Amanda's chagrin, the fourteen students she has requested are not buying in to her lessons. Her first classes are going nowhere. She wonders if this group—the kids whom everyone in the building, including the students themselves, believes cannot or will not learn—has beaten her.

The "solution": Amanda has noted that her students beat out rhythms on the walls as they pass between classes. They drum rhythms with their fingers under the tables of the art room as they refuse to engage with the art materials that she has distributed. On one level, she finds this rejection of the visual materials painful. Like many art teachers, she likes to think of herself as a bit of a shaman with a magical toolkit of visually enticing materials to lure students into education. It hurts to think the toolkit is not working. Yet on the other hand, Amanda can clearly see what holds the students' attention: music. If they will not come to her, then she will go to them.

There is a music department at Gateway Middle, yet Amanda is not certified to teach music. There are state standards for teaching visual art, and Amanda's fourteen students are in a visual arts class. And so, Amanda first goes to the music faculty and asks if they would object if she introduced rap music into her classroom. While a bit baffled with such a request, the music faculty does not object, because rap has no place in the state music standards that guides its teaching. Next, Amanda goes to her principal and vice principal and asks if they would object to the use of singing and dancing in her classroom. The administrators are a bit puzzled, but they reassure her that if she can make sure these fourteen students are not disrupting the rest of the school, she can do whatever she likes inside her classroom.

With these permissions, she begins her new lesson. She asks her students if they will teach her—White Girl—to dance. There is an immediate buzz of excitement in the classroom. Amanda sets out a few parameters. The lyrics must be clean, and each member of the class has to do more than bust his or her own moves. They need to teach the others, including Amanda, how to dance.

The classes proceed with music, dancing, and a great deal of laughter. Occasionally, Amanda asks the class to stop and consider what makes some of the dance moves particularly effective. With some coaxing, the students begin to talk about how gestures communicate, how the body somatically conveys meanings—that is, how bodily movement and position are related to their emotions. As the class proceeds, Amanda asks particularly effective dancers to hold their pose. She then provides large pieces of paper and charcoal so the students can begin to capture on paper how dance expression enables the representation of their emotional states. The students, who just a couple of weeks previously refused to take a drawing tool in their hands or make a mark on paper, now respond with tentative enthusiasm. They have never done anything like this before, but they are intrigued. So Amanda takes a moment to give a few drawing tips. Toward the end of class, she has students display their drawings, and in a group, they talk about the meaning they have captured. This activity creates an opportunity for Amanda to introduce the concepts of metaphor and simile.

As the students continue to dance and draw in response to their music, each drawing becomes its own metaphor. Amanda now introduces the concept of poetry as an extended series of metaphors. The drawings are sketches of individual, expressive, metaphoric elements, and she encourages the students to combine these elements into personal poems. As the students begin to juxtapose, collage, and overlay their linguistic metaphors inspired by their drawings, they make a new discovery: There is something they want to say. For some, poetry is not enough to say everything they feel. Amanda encourages these students to explore their feelings in prose texts.

Some students want to record the dancer with digital video rather than drawing. Amanda has inexpensive pocket cameras for these students to use, and her classroom computer allows students to learn the basics of film editing. Once the students have mastered the technical basics, she allows students to go to the school computer lab, which she has reserved for them to finish their work.

Every day the students begin each class period with music and dancing. The students introduce Amanda to their insider world—hyperconnective youth culture—and they teach her dances that only the hippest of the hipsters know, all the time respecting her mandate to keep the lyrics clean.

At the end of the semester, Amanda organizes an exhibition and a performance for her class to which she invites the students' friends and families as well as other members of the faculty and the school's administration. The students display their drawings and videos, but the evening focuses on their reading from their poems and essays. Amanda wants to highlight these efforts, because these readings are from the students who would not engage with the curriculum, the students other teachers wanted removed from their classrooms because they thought the students could not and would not learn. The culminating event of the evening is Amanda joining the entire class in the latest hip-hop dance.

The rationale for the instruction: In this solution to her teaching dilemma, Amanda's pedagogical tactic transfers authority of expertise to her students. This shift does not come without risk. As noted, at Gateway student-on-student violence is a constant concern. To cede authority to students is a move that many teachers at Gateway are afraid to make.

The second part of letting go of authority requires Amanda to go to a place outside her comfort zone, in this case, with hip-hop dancing. Negotiating her personal discomfort is something that Amanda feels is critical to her ability to connect with marginalized students. She believes that she must avoid sending implicit messages to her students that she disapproves of them or that they intimidate her. She makes a point of visiting students in their homes to demonstrate that she is not afraid to walk the streets of their neighborhoods. Being-in-relationship with these students means meeting them eye-to-eye. This effort too is part of learning to see. Engaging the challenges of perception and eschewing the comforts of recognition are foundational to her discipline.

Questions for Reflection

1. Can you imagine teaching from a place of not knowing? What would it be like to allow your classroom to become a place where you are not the authority?

2. This scenario ends without mentioning how any of these fourteen students did on the Language Arts portion of their next state mandated exam. Does their performance on standardized tests matter for art teachers?

3. In your experience, do schools focus their efforts on students closest to meeting a benchmark and allocate fewer resources to those students who are unlikely to ever pass? How has Amanda addressed this problem? What does she sacrifice from her own professional practice to do this?

4. In what ways has Amanda provided her students with authentic literacy experiences?

5. In what ways can ideas from Amanda's class be applied across the school curriculum?

6. How might Amanda respond to criticisms from parents and colleagues that she has "dumbed down" the class with popular culture, and lowered her own dignity as a teacher by exposing herself to her students' laughter and ridicule?

7. To what degree is this approach compatible with national standards mandates, and how might you modify the activities to fit within requirements you might face in meeting the school's mission to be highly ranked according to test scores?

8. How might Amanda fare on existing teacher evaluation instruments that rate her effectiveness and determine her merit?

9. If existing evaluation instruments are not sensitive to what she accomplishes, what sort of alternative would you propose to provide a more valid means of measuring her effectiveness?

SCENARIO 5: A Literacy of Listening: Relational Aesthetics

The setting: Jerome High School is an urban school facing urban challenges, most of them being rooted in the cycle of poverty in which the students live. The town's major industries have closed up shop and moved their production overseas, leaving many families unemployed and in desperate circumstances. Only 65 percent of students graduate, and 25 percent of the seniors fail the state Language Arts graduation exam the first time they take it. Jerome High is a Title I school with 78 percent of the students eligible for free or reduced-price lunch.

With four grade levels and more than 1,500 students, Jerome consistently fails to meet AYP expectations. This condition allows students to transfer to the other high school in the small district. The only problem with this source of relief is that the other school also fails to meet AYP benchmarks. Therefore, the students, even if they wanted to leave, really have nowhere else to go. As a self-chosen second indicator for AYP, Jerome has challenged itself to achieve an 85 percent graduation rate. It consistently falls beneath this mark.

The characters: Jennie Kim is one of two art teachers at Jerome High. She is in her fifth year of teaching. As a child, she came to the United States from Korea, where her family had lived in desolate poverty. She remembers the single concrete room that the family rented. There was minimal furniture. All the family members slept together on the floor. Running water, the main cooking area, sinks, and toilets were all outside the apartment. She had to enter the open air in the winter to use these facilities. To wash, she had to go outside to get water in a bucket, bring it back to the apartment to heat it on the charcoal stove, and then wash with a basin without privacy in the room. Jennie knows what it means to be poor and she can empathize with the mental, emotional, and physical stress that poverty inflicts on the students she teaches.

The context: Jennie wants her art room to be a haven. Certainly, Jerome High is not a safe harbor that fosters a community of learners. Student-on-student violence is rampant. Aggression is by no means gender specific. The girls can be just as vicious as the boys. On multiple occasions, diminutive Jennie has thrown herself into a brawl of girls to physically restrain the combatants. Many administrators, teachers, and students are just trying to survive, although some teachers, like Jennie, believe that they can close the door to their classroom and in their space, for the limited time of the class period, can make another kind of reality possible for their students.

The dilemma: Jennie's Art II class enrolls twenty-six students. Supplies are limited. The art department's kiln has been broken for years, and the school never seems to have the money to get it fixed. There is not enough money for individual portions of clay. However, Ms. Kim does not want to cut ceramics from her curriculum. She recognizes that molding sensuous clay is a powerful experience. The ability to shape and endlessly reconfigure pliable clay is a metaphor for a lesson that Jennie wants to convey to her students: They have an endless and unlimited ability to reshape themselves. Through clay, she wants to teach her students how to rewrite themselves.

Jennie is inspired by the German artist Joseph Beuys, who argues that the purpose of art is to render a new social sculpture (Borer, 1997). By this, he means that art has to create new ways that individuals within society communicate to the purpose of finding and refining community. An example of this idea was his contribution to the international invitational art exhibition Documenta 5 in 1972. The artwork, *Bureau for Direct Democracy,* consisted of Beuys sitting in a seminar room, all day, every day for the four months the show was open to the public, conducting discussions on art and community with anyone who wanted to sit at the table and join the conversation.

Contemporary art practice that emphasizes experiential moments where the point is how people talk with each other, rather than the visual appreciation of an object, is known as relational aesthetics (Bourriaud, 2002). Jennie sees curricular potential in this type of artwork, as it is based on creating a place—an environment—rather than objects (for which she does not have the supplies). It is a drastic shift from traditional art making, but one that could influence her students more than creating masterpieces.

Jennie also struggles with student attendance. Jerome High School is so desperate for the students to just show up at school that it has abandoned any kind of institutional value that students should appear in class on time. Jerome High, to prevent students from despairing that they have missed too much school and quitting altogether, officially allows students to miss six periods of each of the classes in which they are enrolled without impact on their grade. Thus, students know they have six "Get Out of Class Free" cards per class. Jennie has found that this school policy wreaks havoc on her art curriculum because it undercuts her attempts to build sequential skills. She has no power to penalize students who do not show up for class.

The "solution": As a result of these constraints—lack of supplies, inconsistent attendance, and overall student level of engagement and ability—Jennie turns to relational aesthetics for her lesson in clay. Each of the following three criteria helps combat the problems she is faced with in teaching visual literacy at her school and allows the students to achieve more open-ended solutions to their own art-making problems. Here are her criteria for the Beuys-inspired lesson.

1. *Document daily class time (valuing the process of art creation).* Jennie's lesson requires that students complete three daily tasks. First, students must submit a personal time log at the end of each class. The time log does not tell students what they are supposed to do. Rather, it is a tool to try to help students reflect on what exactly it is that they are doing. To ensure the log is completed, Jennie will pause at moments throughout the class, ask students to note the precise time, and explain what they are currently doing. The time log is Jennie's attempt to instill mindfulness, as she has no power to enforce attendance. Second, after completing their time logs, students reflect in a visual journal. These reflections can include images or writing. They may put sticky notes in the journal or paste clippings from a magazine, but they must attempt to reflect on how they engage during art class. Third, Jennie takes a digital photograph on her cell phone to make a record of what each student is doing. At the end of each day, she prints these photos so that the students will have a visual record of their work.

2. *Work in groups, based on a theme.* Because there is not enough clay for each student to work individually, by necessity the project has to be achieved through group work. The class divides into five groups, and after members have a chance to consult,

they decide collectively that all groups will use their clay to explore the theme of humanity versus nature. Continuing the whole class discussion, the students identify how they can explore issues of survival, shelter, nurture, and weather (although they are not limited to these aspects of survival).

3. *Reuse the materials (art is not stable)*. Each day the students work together with the clay to brainstorm and articulate ideas around their selected topic, and at the end of the class period, each group smashes the clay down again for storage. The only record of what the group has accomplished is the process photographs that Jennie takes and the personal reflections students write in their visual journals. However, these documents successfully record how, in each new class period, the group builds on previous ideas to push its thinking further.

Over the course of three weeks, members within each group negotiate together different conceptual frameworks for their collaborative work and test these ideas in class. Because the group tears down its clay forms daily, it's also possible for groups to revisit the discarded ideas from the previous day. One group decides to make a sequence of tableaus over the three weeks that begin with a totally nurturing natural environment and transition to a totally nurturing human-made environment. These explorations move out of the classroom and onto the adjacent concrete patio to allow the students to use the spigot to introduce water into their thinking. They can now explore issues of irrigation, as well as find additional modeling materials such as rocks, dirt, leaves, and broken branches.

Another group never gets past its disaster movie obsession. Each day there is a new natural disaster that wipes out civilization. However, Jennie requires the group to produce new daily details for its scenarios that feature revised beginnings, middles, and ends.

A third group spends its time diligently rolling out clay snakes, coils of clay made by rocking clay gently between the palm of the hand and the table surface while applying gentle pressure. Rolling clay is generally considered a kindergarten motor skill development task, yet this tactile experience solemnly engages these older students. This group proudly works on its family of "snakes" and creates nurturing tales of how the mother and father snake care for the children.

Arches fascinate the fourth group. This interest sends its members off to the library to find new ways that they can assemble their daily arch construction into new architectural forms. Ultimately, these forms morph into elaborate game pieces. The students spend the last days of the project struggling to create rules for a game that ultimately proves to be incomprehensible, requiring them to rethink and re-explain their rules and thus revise their composition, as they would with their writing.

At the end of the unit, each group creates, on a large block of colored paper, a poster that documents its efforts. Besides featuring the documentary images that the students have made of their process, each student goes through his or her visual journals and reworks an entry to add to the design. Finally, each group presents its work to the class. Jennie is impressed with the enthusiasm with which each group member discusses his or her work. The groups address their processes of collaboration. Furthermore, students listen attentively to other members of class. Students even show up for class and arrive on time. Jennie feels she has successfully achieved, for at least this small moment, a community of learners who can listen and respond to each other.

The rationale for the instruction: Official curriculum standards in the visual arts overwhelmingly privilege the making of objects whose worth is demonstrated by being put on display or submitted to prestigious external events for awards. However, for nearly half a century, cutting-edge work in the international art community has moved away from artists making "stuff." Best practice in this conception refers to the creation of art that inspires dialogue among the people who interact with it. For this lesson, Jennie has needed to think beyond the narrow framework of her secondary visual arts curriculum and work toward a larger idea of what it means to know—to become literate in the visual arts.

Questions for Reflection

1. One of Jennie's groups never gets out of its enthrallment with popular culture and "Big Bang" movies filled with explosions and car chases. Does this group ever engage with art? Does it engage with literacy?

2. How is Jennie defining visual literacy? Compare Jennie's approach with the teachers in other scenarios from this chapter. How is she different? What is consistent across all five of these scenarios?

3. Jennie teaches at a high school where the norms expected by the federal government are difficult to reach or maintain and where behavioral issues often make it hard to teach the prescribed curriculum. What must committed teachers like Jennie do to serve their students in such an environment?

4. Is there any content discipline specific to the visual arts in this lesson? Has Jennie gone totally rogue as a visual arts specialist?

5. Do all students learn at high levels in this lesson?

6. In what ways can ideas from Jennie's class be applied across the school curriculum?

7. To what degree is this approach compatible with national standards mandates, and how might you modify the activities to fit within requirements you might face in meeting the school's mission to be highly ranked according to test scores?

8. How might Jennie fare on existing teacher evaluation instruments that rate her effectiveness and determine her merit?

9. If existing evaluation instruments are not sensitive to what she accomplishes, what sort of alternative would you propose to provide a more valid means of measuring her effectiveness?

REFERENCES

Angulo, A. J. (2012). *Empire and education: A history of greed and goodwill from the War of 1898 to the War on Terror*. New York, NY: Palgrave Macmillan.

Borer, A. (1997). A lament for Joseph Beuys. In L. Schirmer (Ed.), *The essential Joseph Beuys* (pp. 11–34). Cambridge, MA: MIT Press.

Bourriaud, N. (2002). *Relational aesthetics*. Dijon, France: Les Presses du Réel.

Bruner, J. S. (1960). *The process of education*. Cambridge, MA: Harvard University Press.

Dewey, J. (1934). *Art as experience*. New York, NY: Milton, Balch.

Efland, A. (1976). The school art style: A functional analysis. *Studies in Art Education, 17*(2), 37–44.

Eisner, E. W. (2002). *The arts and the creation of mind*. New Haven, CT: Yale University Press.

Feldman, E. (1994). *Practical art criticism*. Englewood Cliffs, NJ: Prentice Hall.

Foucault, M. (1988). *The history of sexuality: Vol. 3. The care of the self* (R. Hurley, Trans.). New York, NY: Vintage.

Freud, S. (1961). *Civilization and its discontents* (J. Strachey, Trans.). New York, NY: Norton. (Original work published 1930)

Georgia Department of Education. (2009). *Georgia performance standards: Visual arts*. Retrieved September 15, 2010, from https://www.georgiastandards.org/Standards/Pages/BrowseStandards/FineArts.aspx

Goel, T. (2011, August 5). Haiti: Showcase of imperialist exploitation. *LiberationNews.org*. Retrieved from http://www.pslweb.org/liberationnews/news/haiti-showcase-of.html

Greene, M. (2001). *Variations on a blue guitar: The Lincoln Center Institute lectures on aesthetic education*. New York, NY: Teachers College Press.

Loewen, J. W. (1996). *Lies my teacher told me: Everything your American history textbook got wrong*. New York, NY: Touchstone.

Lowenfeld, V. (1947). *Creative and mental growth*. New York, NY: Macmillan.

Murray, D. M. (1996). *Crafting a life in essay, story, poem*. Portsmouth, NH: Heinemann.

Noddings, N. (1995). Teaching themes of care. *Phi Delta Kappan, 76*(9), 675–679.

Rorty, R. (1989). *Contingency, irony, and solidarity*. Cambridge, UK: Cambridge University Press.

Rosenblatt, L. M. (2005). *Making meaning with texts: Selected essays*. Portsmouth, NH: Heinemann.

Wachowiak, F., & Clements, R. D. (2001). *Emphasis art: A qualitative art program for elementary and middle schools* (7th ed.). New York, NY: Longman.

NOTES

1. Embedded in this philosophy was an insistence on seeing the art teacher as dealing with children, not with students. Art education stood apart from, and was often in opposition to, other forms of learning within school.
2. For an example, see the Georgia Visual Arts Performance Standards at www.georgiastandards.org/standards/Pages/BrowseStandards/FineArts.aspx (Georgia Department of Education, 2009).

3. An art teacher might follow Feldman's (1994) method of critiquing a piece of art. The method encourages students to linger with the piece, looking carefully at the elements (describing), thinking about how those elements work together to share a message (analyzing), extracting symbols or other meanings that are historically or culturally present (interpreting), and deciding on the personal response to the piece (judging).

4. The authors are not suggesting that teachers send their students to this website, as some of the content might be considered inappropriate for students; instead, teachers wishing to replicate this unit might provide students with similar examples that meet their school's standards for propriety.

5. Since its inception, Warren has received hundreds of secrets each week, and he now maintains a website (www.postsecret.com) where he makes weekly posts of the best new secrets that are submitted to him. He has published five books drawing work from this archive. The authors of this chapter are not suggesting that teachers send their students to this website, as some of the content might be considered inappropriate for students; instead, teachers wishing to replicate this unit might provide students with similar examples that meet their school's standards for propriety.

6. The IB curriculum emphasizes inquiry-based learning and recognizes the role of the arts in holistic education. It also encourages student reflection and the development of the IB learner profile where students strive to be knowledge-able, principled, open-minded, caring, balanced, and reflective risk-takers, thinkers, communicators, and inquirers (see www.ibo.org).

6 Music and Drama Literacies

Katherine D. Strand and Gus Weltsek

I n this chapter, we will explore topics and challenges in teaching literacy within the disciplines of music and drama. The literacy skills required in the two disciplines are quite different, so the chapter is separated into two sections. We invite you, however, to consider similarities and differences between the two in terms of the suggested instructional content and pedagogical approaches.

MUSIC LITERACY

It is impossible to explore music literacy without being reminded of the aphorisms associated with music. Adages such as "Music is a universal language" (anonymous) and "Music expresses that which cannot be said and on which it is impossible to be silent" (attributed to Victor Hugo) articulate the deep-seated belief that music has semantic and emotive qualities that make it simultaneously the same as, and different from, verbal communication. Literacy in performed music has characteristics similar to that of performed language (Garton & Pratt, 1998). However, written music also has characteristics that, although similar to literacy in language, include symbols to inform the reader of the score about the semantics of performance.

Teaching for music literacy has traditionally been considered a part of a pedagogy based upon musical performance: Learners are instructed to read a system of notation and perform music within a Western art tradition. In recent years, alternative views of literacy and musicianship have resulted in attention to informal music-making practices (those most often found outside school settings), musical creativity, and alternate systems of notation. This section will outline the characteristics of music literacy and end with a scenario that poses conundrums typical to literacy instruction in public schools. By examining deeply the characteristics of the traditional and newer variations on musical literacy, we will compare music literacy with other disciplines in terms of both the logic behind the symbol systems and the symbols themselves.

AURAL DISCRIMINATION AND READING MUSIC

Music literacy has traditionally been understood to mean the ability to *discriminate* between various tonal and rhythmic ideas and to *read* Western music notation. This belief is evinced by Gordon's *Iowa Test of Music Literacy* (1970). These tests are divided into two sections, Rhythmic Concepts and Tonal Concepts, each including testing for aural discrimination, reading notation, and performing notation.

Literacy in terms of aural discrimination is taught through *ear training*. In increasing levels of difficulty, students learn to identify, label, and perform notational ideas:

- high versus low pitches,
- the direction of a melodic line,
- intervals (the distances between pitches),
- pitches in relation to a tonal center,
- types of scale used in a melody,
- chords by type and position,
- chords in relation to a tonal center,
- chord progressions (chords in patterns), and
- cadences (chord progressions that end melodic phrases).

Audiation, additionally, requires the learner to accomplish all of the above while looking at musical notation. Audiation refers to the ability to hear and comprehend a piece of music when the sound is not physically present (Gordon, 1988).

This nexus between spoken word and music suggests that instruction in one discipline may improve literacy in another. Robert Jourdain (1997) discusses the related systems of language and music and the implications for facilitative roles between the two: Language "represents the contents of the outside world in a symbolic way" (p. 293), while music can "reenact experience within the body, mimicking experience by carefully replicating the temporal patterns of interior feeling in a world of turbulent flow" (p. 296). Western notation literacy itself requires several skill sets.

Chief among them is the ability to read *graphic representations of time and pitch* from left to right and, on a page, from top to bottom. The five lines of a musical staff provide specific information about pitches in a melodic line. The *clef sign* appearing at the beginning of each staff informs the reader about the placement of the five-lined staff upon a grand staff of all pitches available to the human voice. For example, the treble clef 𝄞 indicates relatively higher pitch, or treble voice. Clef signs can also indicate the placement of the pitch labeled *C*. Unlike in English language reading, the notation reader will view one, two, or as many staves as can fit on a page, all of which may sound simultaneously.

Signature signs indicate tonal and pulse relationships among the notes on the score. A *key signature,* for example, indicates how close each note is to the others and the type of scale, or *mode* (major, minor, etc.). Each mode denotes a set of pitches with a formula of intervals that become the building blocks for melodies. The notation reader should also be able to determine which note is the *tonal center* of a melody. The tonal center is the note which, when the melody moves away, causes the hearer to feel tension and, when moving toward and ending on the note, causes the hearer to feel a release of tension (a feeling of "home"). A notation reader should be able to read the tension and release of any notated melodic line.

Historically, different modes are *felt* in very different ways. In *The Republic,* Plato argued that music in each mode would incline listeners and performers alike toward specific behaviors associated with it. He recommended that soldiers should listen only to music in those modes that would make them grow stronger and should avoid modes that would soften them or cause debauchery. He argued as well that changing the modes used in the music of the state would cause social revolt (Plato, Rep. III.10–III.12, 398C–403C). While music scholars no longer hold to the belief that melodies in specific modes will alter behavior, the mode is one of the culturally accepted determiners of musical mood. For example, Halloween music is most often written in Aeolean, or minor, mode. Flamenco is often written in Phrygian mode (considered "fiery"), Irish music uses Mixolydian mode for royalty, and movie scores often include the "ethereal" Lydian mode to accompany scenes with fairies, elves, or nirvana.

Western music tends to have an underlying pulse, or beat. *Time signature* indicates the relative speed of an *underlying steady pulse* of the melody and then the pattern of *strong and weak beats.* A 4/4 time signature refers to a walking-speed pulse in the pattern strong-weak-weak-weak, reinforced by the bar lines that remind the musical score reader when to perform the next note with a strong pulse. The time signature further tells the reader something important about the way the music should *move.* Common time *feels* like a march, whereas a time signature of 3/4 *feels* like a dance (a waltz, specifically), and 6/8 *feels* like rocking or swaying as in a lullaby. Different rhythms within these time signatures carry different physical sensations as well.

The perception of rhythmic energy, drive, or forward motion can be as effective on people as melodic mode. Research in music therapy revealed that children with autism responded and were aided by music with a strong steady pulse (Nordoff & Robbins, 1977). Rhythmic chants are similarly found to boost energy, as evidenced in sports arenas, work songs, and wherever a crowd supports an individual facing a challenge. A performer reading notation must perform the intended rhythmic energy and forward motion while reading a score.

Additional symbols within notation reading fall into two categories:

1. Those that direct the reader *around the musical score,* such as repeat signs, *da capo al coda* ("go back to the beginning and read once again until the coda sign"), or *dal segno* ("repeat from the last sign passed in the score")

2. Those that direct the reader in the *expressive qualities,* such as *dolce* (sweetly), *allegro* (moderately fast), and *pianissimo* (very quietly)

Beyond the ability to read and perform the notes and rhythms, music literacy involves knowledge of the historical and cultural performance practices. Music of different time periods should also be read and performed in different ways. Music from the Classical period should stress regularity, symmetry, and gentility, while music of the Baroque and Romantic eras should stress emotional energies and asymmetry. Latin jazz employs specific rhythmic and harmonic gestures that are meant to sound differently than do those of hip-hop.

Because of all the felt qualities in music performance, Western musical scores express several different musical languages. In principle, musical literacy should reach a level of fluency where the reader is able to pick up a multistaffed musical score and hear all of the parts together. For example, see Figure 6.1 to "hear" the opening of Beethoven's Fifth Symphony. The musician's performance of the notation should be developed beyond identification into the ability to add all of the expressive *felt* qualities written into the musical score, indicated by the date and composer of the composition, and/or intended by the performer.

ALTERNATE MUSICAL LITERACIES

Literacy within the Western notation system, for all of its capabilities, is still problematic. It is possible, for example, to be literate in a musical

Figure 6.1 The Opening of Ludwig Van Beethoven's Symphony No. 5, First Movement

notation system without being able to perform (communicate) the intended music. Aural discrimination by itself does not guarantee that a performer can interpret a musical score. More important, the Western notation system was developed to capture the sense of movement, energy, texture, and structures of European music. As such, it is ill equipped to communicate non-Western musical traditions or changes to the felt qualities of musical expression. As the composer Libby Larsen explained,

> I believe that musical artifacts emerge from the very heart of our culture. Our culture has developed music around our own vernacular language. Rock and roll is one example, and gospel another. Ragtime is a mix of Western European and the natural rhythms of our language. Motion, not just pulse, is a cultural creation. The way

that I think about motion indicates that we in music education may be impoverishing our students, specifically in our ability to hear ourselves in the real motion in music. Whenever we teach young people about music by using meters and counting, which are not organic to how we naturally speak or move, we disconnect the symbol systems created to codify and communicate from real music. (quoted in Strand & Larsen, 2011, p. 60)

Further, music education systems of the past hundred years have not incorporated *creating* music. Therefore, although learners are taught to be literate in reading notation, they are not taught how to express their own musical ideas (Strand, 2006).

Both the forms of literacy and the symbol systems have come under question in recent years. Musical literacy has been altered by access to and developments in technology, by new attention to informal learning practices, and by developing awareness of literacy practices in other cultures. Green (2001, 2008) examined the practices and learning strategies of popular musicians, concluding that literacy in these communities of practice was based upon enculturation through immersion in the music-making practices and improvisation. Musical literacy is thus not considered separate from the bodily experience and creative music making. Green's work suggests that the *kinesthetic experience* is as important as audiation for musical literacy.

Bamberger (1995) and Upitis (1992) conducted independent examinations of young children's invented notation systems, finding that graphic symbol systems take different forms, depending on the child's perception of the music in question. Bamberger found that there were developmental trends based upon perception and internal pulse keeping, which suggests that preschoolers may benefit from the use of *rebuses.* School-aged children, on the other hand, spontaneously notated a pulse with their invented systems. Upitis found that when children were allowed to compose and create their own *invented notation,* they were better able to negotiate the more formalized traditional notation system.

Technological advances have allowed people to use their own personal vocabulary of *bodily gestures* to make music. Machover (2002) and the other researchers at the Massachusetts Institute of Technology have developed programs such as Hyperstudio that allow users to compose multilayered works using a lettered keyboard and mouse, and then use gestures to "conduct" the performance, effectively using gesture as a literacy practice. *Piano roll notation* in many music programs allows the reader to interpret a visual representation including colors, longer and shorter lines, and pitch represented higher on the computer screen. In short, these tools allow for an iconic representation of rhythm, pitch, texture, and tone color, which produces a new "grammar" of personalized musical gestures.

In sum, musical literacy cannot be considered apart from the context of the musical experience and community, the age of the child, the form of the musical experience, or the symbol systems that are created or interpreted for a musical experience. New literacies, involving alternative and invented notation and personalized or enculturated musical gestures, indicate that some revision is needed in music literacy instruction.

SCENARIO

SCENARIO 1: Musical Literacy With Informal Learning Practices

The setting: An urban elementary school. About 80 percent of the students receive free lunch, with another 5 percent qualifying for reduced-price lunch. Fifty percent of the students are European American, 15 percent are African American, 30 percent are Latino/a, and 5 percent are mixed race. The school uses a dual immersion bilingual program, which means that each class of children is taught for half of the school day by a teacher who speaks English and the other half of the day by a teacher who speaks Spanish, with the students learning the same curriculum in the two languages.

The characters: Annelle Grabowski is the music teacher. Annelle has been trained in a music conservatory and is a pianist. As an itinerant teacher, she has a cart for her music materials as she travels from room to room to teach, transferring the cart's contents to a bag for her forays to classes on the second floor. The school principal, Dr. Maribel Lond, taught primary school children for twenty-two years before completing her doctorate and moving into school administration. She played piano as a child but abandoned playing music in her teens. She continued, however, to love and collect music throughout her teen and adult life. Further, in taking dance classes as a young woman, she experienced the relation between sound and motion, leading her to see music as not just an aural experience but one that is often integrated with other modes of expression, a relation that she began to notice in film soundtracks and other cultural forms of art.

The context: Maribel has received word from the school board that schools should include integrated curricula, an idea they derived from their exposure to Reggio Emilia Schools, the Italian-based educational approach based on the maxims that children should

- have some control over the direction of their learning,
- learn through exploratory multisensory experience,
- learn through relationships with other children,
- have myriad opportunities to express themselves in multiple ways,
- be taught by teachers who themselves are positioned as colearners, and
- be supported heavily by their parents in their education.

Maribel has, in response, decided that music should be integrated into the curriculum, not taught as a stand-alone subject. She has told Annelle that she must collaborate with the classroom teachers in order to integrate music into each classroom's instruction.

The principal has also stressed that the springtime accountability testing is of utmost importance, since the school moved out of the "failing school" category only recently. She has told the classroom teachers that preparation for the tests is their highest priority. The teachers, for their part, are frustrated with earlier starts to the school year, frozen salaries, and cuts in the budget for supplies. All teachers have one half-period for lunch and a full period for planning, which they take when the children have special subjects: music, gym, computer keyboarding, and art. The special subject teachers in turn have a planning period during the first forty-five minutes of each school day.

The school has been successful with their bilingual program. By the third grade, most of the children can read, write, and speak in both English and Spanish. Annelle has learned to teach several songs in Spanish. She has included music from Mexico, Brazil, Cuba, and Poland for the children to perform. Annelle has also taken a workshop on ESL/ENL instruction, learning techniques such as Total Physical Response (TPR) developed by James Asher, which relies on code-breaking strategies for learning language combined with physical movement.

The dilemma: Annelle has to find a way to collaborate with each classroom teacher in the school, while meeting state and national standards for teaching musical literacy and providing high-quality musical experiences. Annelle does not share a planning period with any of the other teachers, but she does have a lunch period with a few of them. Some of the classroom teachers are uncomfortable in taking their lunch time to work with Annelle, and they express frustration that they must use valuable classroom time for what some consider the "frill" of music.

Annelle wants to satisfy the principal and the requests that the classroom teachers make, but she also needs to orchestrate student performances for the fall and spring Parent-Teacher Association meetings, and she has an April "Celebration of the Arts" to plan and prepare.

The "solution": By October, Annelle has gone to each classroom teacher several times, but the results have been disappointing because she has had to do all of the planning in response to grade level teachers' lessons. For example, when she learned that the first-grade class would be working with "trains, buses, and other locomotion" in September, Annelle developed a unit on higher and lower pitch to illustrate the Doppler effect. She also taught the children songs such as "The Wheels on the Bus" and played music within the travel theme, such as Billy Strayhorn's *Take the A Train.* These activities were enjoyable for everyone, but Annelle felt that she had to cobble together instruction in order to address musical literacy in her music lessons. She did not feel satisfied that either she or the students made real connections between the literacy studies in the classroom and musical literacy.

During the winter, Annelle develops some lessons for the first grade to help students become more adept in their explorations of expressive musical qualities such as loud/soft, fast/slow, smooth/bouncy, and so forth. Her goal is to combine musical and language literacy skills. She creates some lessons that use TPR. In groups of three, children speak, move, and improvise on small xylophones with the following sentences:

I woke up this morning

I jumped out of bed.

I brushed my teeth.

I slipped into my shoes.

I ate my breakfast.

I walked to school.

By practicing speaking with physical movements and musical sound, the students become more confident in their English language skills. By combining musical exploration with TPR, Annelle is then able to introduce expressive musical terms through familiar words and movements.

During the same quarter, the second-grade teacher provides Annelle with a poem about a frog, since the class is learning about amphibians.

Frog, he jumps with all his might

Mighty flight, in the light

Frog, he splashes in the bog

Soggy frog, in the fog

Frog, he catches bugs to eat

Tasty treat, bugs for meat

Frog, he never shuts his eyes

No surprise, tiny eyes

Annelle sees the opportunity to teach this pattern-based poem by emphasizing rhythmic notation. She develops a lesson where the students invent their own notation systems for different instrument sounds they choose to represent each of the rhyming words. While these last two activities allow Annelle to teach musical literacy, she still feels that there are deeper connections between disciplines that would make learning more meaningful for the students and more fulfilling for the teachers.

Later that year, she is finally able to make such connections. As she walks into the second-grade classroom one day in midwinter, she finds that the classroom teacher is frustrated because the students are not picking up on reading timelines.

Annelle asks to use the timeline drawn on the board. She draws a half note over the year 2000, then two quarter notes over the years 2010 and 2015. She asks the students to clap the rhythm, as she taught them to do in first grade. Then she asks what would happen if the music were very slow. They clap the rhythm again but count to ten after the half note and to five after the quarter notes. Finally, she asks what would happen if the music were so slow that it took a week between the first and second notes. The students respond that they could clap only once that day and then wait until the next music class.

Challenging them, she asks when they could clap the third note. The students figure that they could clap on Tuesday, since their music classes are on Fridays. Dutifully, they clap once while Annelle points to the half note, then once again when she enters the classroom the next week, and once more when she pops her head in the doorway on Tuesday the following week. Both she and the classroom teacher express surprise: The students have never made the connection between reading notation and reading a timeline before.

Still later in the year, Annelle and an eighth-grade Language Arts teacher plan to teach a unit on music and poetry. In a lunchtime conversation, they discover similar ideas between twentieth-century concrete poetry and twentieth-century invented notation forms. They cocreate a unit to have students compare traditional poetry and musical notation with the twentieth-century developments. Working together, they find that the students are able to comprehend and create in both disciplines. Even more surprising, the teachers find that they enjoy comparing their disciplines in order to find commonalities and differences.

The rationale for the instruction: Maribel believed strongly that integrated arts instruction would deepen student learning and would enhance the retention of information. This insight was borne out in some of the collaborations between Annelle and some of the grade-level teachers, as well as in some of her own imaginative instruction. Musical literacy, she found, has characteristics similar to literacy in many other areas.

Questions for Reflection

1. What other musical learning tools can be used to help the children in this school become more proficient in speaking English and Spanish?

2. What additional content connections exist between teaching musical literacy and teaching literacy in English learning? Language Arts? Math? Life Sciences? Social Sciences? Other areas of the curriculum?

3. What additional pedagogical connections can be drawn between teaching musical literacy and teaching these other disciplines?

4. In what ways can an integrated curriculum for teaching literacy help prepare students to perform well on standardized tests?

5. If a school includes students from cultures that use musical conventions from outside the Western tradition, to what degree is the teacher responsible for including additional musical forms in the curriculum?

6. If you were evaluating Annelle and the year's integration efforts, what criteria would you use to assess her teaching, and how would you rate her instruction?

DRAMA LITERACY

Morrell (2002) argues that "often, the failure of urban students to develop 'academic' literacy skills stems not from a lack of intelligence but from the inaccessibility of the school curriculum to students who are not in the 'dominant' or 'mainstream' culture" (p. 72). Morrell's statement resonates with the notion that the experiential knowledge that the students use in their personal literacy practices is not represented in the academic curriculum. The result of this absence is that these everyday literacy practices are not found in what is being taught or tested in school.

The contemporary United States educational climate is focused upon standard assessments and evaluation. It tends to discourage pedagogies that harness the natural creative ability and the personal literacy practices that students bring to the educational table in favor of those that are believed to teach to a common knowledge base. However, as Au and Valencia (2010) argue when writing about standards-based education, "Research over the past 10 years has clearly demonstrated that a variety of instructional strategies, teacher practices . . . have been found in successful schools, especially those that have underperformed" (p. 4). Through the infusion of Drama and Theater Education, as *multimodal, transmediated* literacy practices, it is possible to engage students' personal literacy practices while introducing standards-based educational objectives and curriculum, and high-stakes, testable skills.

WHY AND HOW DOES DRAMA WORK?

There are many current and very relevant ideas that help in the understanding of exactly what drama enables. Among these are *situated literacy studies, multimodal literacy,* and *transmediation* theories. By situated literacy (Barton & Hamilton, 2000), we mean literacy teaching approaches that take into account the cultural variables that play into student literacy learning. Heath (1986) notes that this type of "cultural learning includes all the learning that enables a member of a family and a community to behave appropriately within that group, which is critical to one's self identification and whose approval is necessary for self-esteem" (p. 146).

Using this approach, classroom teachers create learning environments and lessons that support students' use of culturally situated literacy practices and ways of contextualizing knowledge as a means to interpret and connect with the structures of school literacy learning and testing. In this instruction, teachers do not discourage the student's already-formed cultural literacy practices, such as first languages or the many practices available through a New Literacies approach (New London Group, 1996): texting, gaming, twittering, and using other media available on electronic devices. Rather, teachers see what students bring to school as cognitively congruent with and intellectually vital to the learning of school literacies, even as the conventions of their everyday social expression often depart from those expected in school.

The next component in understanding why and how drama works is the concept of multimodal literacy studies. Siegel (2006) grounds multimodality in semiotics, "an interdisciplinary field of studies that examines how meaning is made through signs of all kinds—pictures, gestures, music—not just words" (p. 65; cf. Smagorinsky, 2001). In everyday interactions, students read and create visual images, speak, and take on various roles in their relationships in diverse settings. In doing so, they typically use gestures and body positions to convey emotions and engage in other meaning-laden forms of communication.

Each of these literacy practices is intimately connected, each supporting the other in a dance of meaning-making. Harste, Woodward, and Burke (1984) found that "talking, gesturing, dramatizing, and drawing are 'an intimate and integral part' of the writing process" (cited in Siegel, 2006, p. 13). Moreover, Fueyo (1991) observed that students supported through a multimodal approach could become better aware of and improve their use of sign systems, including, but not limited to, drawing, music, drama, and technology. Fueyo also discovered that students' use and interpretation of multiple sign systems creates an intersection and overlap that strengthens and supports reading and writing ability, findings that Siegel (2006) notes "were particularly important for students labeled at risk for literacy failure" (p. 71). In a multimodal literacy approach, teachers create classroom environments and lessons that use multiple sign systems including reading, writing, music, drama, visual arts, and other disciplines to more fully engage the entirety of students' preexisting culturally situated literacy practices.

Transmediation is a process that involves the "translation of content from one sign system into another" (Suhor, 1984, p. 250), such as when students read a poem and put it to music, or represent its action and meaning through art, or perform it through oral interpretation. The process of transmediation involves the learner in an imaginative reconstruction of a text through another medium. In doing so, the learner typically goes beyond the literal and undertakes acts of analysis, interpretation, and meaning-making. A well-devised drama event does just that, engaging the entire person—mind, body, and experiences that inform the performance— and various props, costumes, and other ways of representing meaning. This approach asks participants to use a variety of sign systems to make meaning of any one fictionalized moment.

SCENARIO

SCENARIO 2: Infused Drama Theater Education Strategies as Multimodal Transmediated Literacy Practices

The setting: From 2005 to 2008, led by Mr. Carmine Tabone, the Educational Arts Team (EAT) partnered with the Jersey City Public Schools on a U.S. Department of Education Arts-in-Education Model Development and Dissemination Grant to improve the Language Arts skills of students in fifty-six fourth- through seventh-grade classrooms (EAT, 2008–2011). The grant further was dedicated to helping teachers incorporate the arts into the curriculum. The EAT used multiple drama- and theater-infused strategies with twenty-eight classes of sixth- and seventh-grade students. The grant further devoted twelve hours of professional development to assist teachers with learning performance-based instructional strategies.

The lessons were built around the places where the language arts and theater arts intersected:

- scenery design and setting;
- acting and characters;
- directing;
- theme, plot, and character relationships;
- scriptwriting; and
- dialogue. (Tabone, 2010)

These lessons created spaces for students to explore the core novels that were being used in the Jersey City Public Schools. These stories included

- Karen Cushman's *The Midwife's Apprentice*
- George Orwell's *Animal Farm*
- Linda Sue Park's *A Single Shard*
- Jerry Spinelli's *Maniac Magee*
- Theodore Taylor's *The Cay*

The characters: English Language Arts teacher Tamiqua Bonder and her seventh-grade English Language Arts class.

The context:

- Due to consistently low standardized tests scores, the district has been labeled repeatedly failing. Several of the schools, including Tamiqua's, are slated to be closed and reopened under strict governmental oversight.
- The superintendent of the district is desperately searching for methods that will increase student literacy achievement on state standardized tests. She is very aware that the traditional methods that have been implemented in the district are not working. The superintendent is also very aware of the research emerging on the value of an arts-infused curriculum on student engagement across the curriculum and within civil responsibility.
- Tamiqua has been selected by the superintendent to participate in the EAT's study. The research is designed to study the effects of infusing drama and theater-rich strategies into her daily Language Arts lessons over a period of one year. Tamiqua has no choice but to participate. Not only must Tamiqua allow EAT members into her classroom and integrate their strategies into her year's lessons, but she must also attend twelve hours of professional development workshops (which she is contractually obligated to do anyway) and then integrate and implement the drama- and theater-rich strategies into her classroom herself.
- Although the state curriculum has standards for Language Arts curriculum that Tamiqua must follow, there are no such standards for drama and theater.
- The community has a great suspicion of the use of arts in the classroom, and she is confronted with a great deal of resistance from caregivers and her immediate supervisors as to the efficacy and potential for the EAT's curriculum.
- Tamiqua's current curriculum is based upon a commercial boxed set reading and writing program.
- Tamiqua has no formal training, experience, or background with the arts or the use of the arts within teaching and learning, and specifically no experience with drama and theater.

The dilemma: Tamiqua, although working under the superintendent's guidance, needs to overcome her own hesitations, suspicions, and ideological and pedagogical struggles with the application of the EAT's drama and theater–infused Language Arts curriculum. She must also navigate the resistance and complications presented by the expectations of her students, the students' caregivers, and her colleagues and administration as she moves out of the existing curriculum. Ultimately, Tamiqua wants to provide the best possible education for her students to succeed, particularly those who have been traditionally marginalized, underserved, and underrepresented in the curriculum.

The "solution": Tamiqua begins by reading extensively about arts-infused literacy. In conjunction with her reading, she engages in multiple conversations with her colleagues, her students, the students' caregivers, the superintendent, and members of the EATs. Through this exploration, she chooses to fully invest and "buy into" the infusion of drama and theater–based literacy methods into her classroom. She feels that, based upon her research and conversations, these strategies hold a great deal of possibility for the students to authentically engage in the exploration of their own unique perceptions of the world. This instruction will work in conjunction with the standards-based, testable curriculum that she is mandated to teach.

Tamiqua decides to begin with an infused lesson that combines the elements of Language Arts through the elements found in theater performance. The strategy called "A View From Your Seat" focuses upon students' learning that novels and plays have themes. The strategy further emphasizes how readers, as well as theater directors, need to explore those themes to understand the book or develop the production.

A View From Your Seat. For this activity, Tamiqua introduces a series of statements that require the students to reflect on their personal lives as a means to express their positions. They indicate their responses by remaining in their seats (disagreeing), sitting with their hands raised (not sure), standing up (agreeing), or standing up with their hand in the air (strongly agreeing). The statements she presents to the students include these:

- Students should pay for their own school books.
- Schools should not bother teaching history.
- Cell phones should be allowed in school.
- School uniforms should be mandatory.
- Parents should be required to volunteer at school for one day a week.
- Summer vacation should be shortened to two weeks.

As the activity proceeds, she asks students to explain why they have chosen their particular point of view, and she encourages each student's position. For example, for the statement that "Summer vacation should be shortened to two weeks," a student strongly disagrees by saying, "I work hard during the school year and need some time to relax and do other things." Tamiqua then reinforces the statement by saying, "Yes, you need to relax and cultivate other interests." Her role serves to help students extend or challenge their thinking and points of view regardless of their position on the topic.

At this point, the strategy engages the students by having them choose a position that requires personal reflection and the interpretation of lived experiences. They also engage in what Bolton (1984) terms "analogous reflection" in drama—that is, a responsibility to deconstruct and reconstruct reality while engaged in the construction of any drama event. The students cannot base their discussion of the topic solely on school-based literacy practices or institutionalized knowledge sets. Rather, the students need to use their past and present understanding of how various sign systems, particularly voice and body, might be used and interpreted as they stand, sit, or raise their hands to take a stance on the topic statement.

When the students intellectually consider a premise such as "Summer vacation should be shortened to two weeks," they engage in transmediation as they are challenged to deconstruct what they hear (an audio sign) into an opinion needing physical representation (a physical sign). This new text is then again reinterpreted as Tamiqua asks them to turn that physical interpretation into a vocal utterance (oral sign). The multimodal transmediated event proceeds from audio, to physical, to oral meaning-making and draws on personal experience as the base for the interpretation. This personal foundation allows students to become more aware of their agency in the literacy process. Students thus become more active and self-regulated learners, which in turn enables them to become more engaged with the curriculum with a greater sense of purpose.

Dramatic Viewpoints. Tamiqua recognizes that the theater arts infusion process depends upon expanding and supporting student discoveries through scaffolding the complexity of the drama strategies. She plans to provide this support by linking one strategy to the next in logical, progressive, and ever more intellectually expansive and challenging ways that prompt students to draw on previous reflections and engagements. Consequently, she decides to introduce the Dramatic Viewpoints strategy following the View From Your Seat activity. Tamiqua now creates a small theater space in front of the classroom, setting up one chair in front of the class and keeping four additional chairs available for later use as the strategy develops. She explains how people play different kinds of roles in life, and the class brainstorms to create a list of such roles, including teacher, student, brother, sister, mother, father, child, adult, friend, enemy, doctor, servant, employer, employee, bully, victim, and other personas.

Next, Tamiqua tells the class that the empty chair in front of the classroom will represent a neutral position; the remaining chairs will be used to seat characters who have a firm position on a statement one way or the other. For instance, these characters might include a principal, a superintendent, a high-achieving student, a low-achieving student, a parent, and so forth. Referring to the previous activity, she asks what character would favor the statement "Summer vacation should be shortened."

Next, students take turns suggesting roles, a step that requires using oral literacy. Based on the statement that the student (in character) expresses, Tamiqua places the student in a seat to the right ("agree") or left ("disagree") of the neutral chair and asks the student to explain why the character being portrayed has taken that position. Students then make a statement as if they were that character. For example, the student who selects the role of the school principal says, "My students forget too much during the summer. How will I ever improve my school's test scores?" Another student selects the part of a teacher who thinks that the school year is already too long and that longer breaks are necessary for everyone to relax and recharge. A third student decides to play the role of the owner of a summer camp who thinks his business would be ruined if school took up part of the summer. Here, too, Tamiqua affirms and reinforces all of the positions. For instance, to the "superintendent" she says, "The school year is much too short. How can the teachers get everything done that needs to be covered? How can you increase test scores?"

Students who are unable to state a clear position receive help from other members of the class. As a way to introduce formal written literacy response, Tamiqua also invites the class to take notes on what each of these characters says.

Throughout this strategy, the students are involved in socially constructed notions of role formation. As they move from one sign system to the next—from the audio, to the physical, to the oral—and as they became more critically aware of the ways in which they individually and collectively interpret the dynamic of power and privilege between the various roles, they explore possible interpretations, positions, and tensions among characters. In other words, through the transmediation from one sign system to the next, from one literacy practice to the next, the students engage in intense critical character interpretation.

Persuasive writing. In order to bring focus to the target modality, writing, and fully connect to curricular needs, Tamiqua also decides to introduce subject material through mini-lessons. For example, after the Dramatic Viewpoints activity, she directs the students to use the notes they have taken to write a letter to one of the characters with whom they disagree. Students must include as many reasons as possible to explain why their own position is the right one. In this way, they use both letter writing and persuasive writing skills. Because Tamiqua wants to fully exploit the benefits of a transmediated multimodal approach to literacy education, she asks the students to read their letters to a partner. Finally, some students share their letters with the group. This feedback then leads to revision in order to develop the students' ability to address opposing arguments when attempting to persuade.

Connecting drama strategies directly to a novel. Through her workshop training, Tamiqua learns that to help students unite their out-of-school literacies with school literacy practices, the theater arts infusion process requires the introduction of a subject text into the lesson. To connect one strategy to the next—and so to maintain, support, and expand student-generated understanding and engagement with the material—she returns to an earlier strategy and scaffolds the complexity by adding textual dimensions.

For example, she decides to replay the View From Your Seat strategy, using a statement that connects with a novel that the class is working on. The students already know how the activity works and how it draws on their own ways of thinking. There is a certain amount of comfort based on this familiarity, and this comfort allows the students greater freedom in exploring and expressing their opinions when the impetus stems from an academic text. To plan the lesson, Tamiqua considers the following statements, which correlate with moments from the five novels that are used in the Jersey City project:

- *The Midwife's Apprentice:* You should help other people, even if they have been unfair to you.
- *Animal Farm:* The government should lie, if necessary, to keep all the people safe.
- *A Single Shard:* Stealing is always wrong.

- *Maniac Magee:* All homeless people, especially children, should be forced to live in shelters.
- *The Cay:* If a person is in trouble, you should do whatever it takes to help.

Returning to the Dramatic Viewpoints strategy, she decided to prompt the class to explore one of these statements by setting up a neutral empty chair and asking students to take positions agreeing and disagreeing with the statement. Then they consider which characters from the novel might have different positions on the statement. As before, Tamiqua affirms and reinforces each character's positions.

The rationale for the instruction: The main benefit of infusing drama strategies into the curriculum is that it allows for the transmediation of ideas through multiple sign systems. Moving from the performed character in the Dramatic Viewpoints into the written letter provides students with an opportunity to explore and make meaning using voice, body, and written modalities. Each step grows from the next and is situated in the students' own personal understanding of the moment. Within the drama-based exploration, the students are not asked for "the" definitive answer, but they are rather encouraged to explore *a* possible answer that is directly, intimately, and uniquely theirs. In this way, Tamiqua provides students with a space to use personal literacy practices (ways of making meaning of the world) in direct relation to school-based literacy challenges such as persuasive letter writing.

By infusing drama strategies into the curriculum, Tamiqua helps the students move in and out of modalities. In doing so, she challenges the students to think through their understanding of how to use multiple sign systems in a variety of ways. The process of transmediation helps them to make meaning through the perceived needs of the drama strategy, the structure of the classroom, and their experiences and knowledge about the world at large.

Questions for Reflection

1. In what ways has Tamiqua's use of drama and theater–infused literacy strategies created spaces for students to bring their own personal literacy practices into the learning environment?

2. How has the inclusion of the students' personal literacy practices allowed Tamiqua to introduce the standardized Language Arts curriculum into the learning environment in meaningful, critical, and authentic ways?

3. What distinct, obvious, and concrete connections are made between the use of drama and theater as an infused literacy learning strategy, student personal literacy practices, and the standards-based Language Arts curriculum?

4. How do the intersections and departures between drama and theater performance and the Language Arts curriculum enable students to become more engaged in the exploration of both forms through personally located systems of meaning-making?

5. What are some of the challenges and complications that may arise from approaching Language Arts learning and literacy achievement through the use of a drama and theater–infused pedagogy?

6. What augmentations, extensions, and/or modification might you envision as means to enhance the relevance of this type of work within your understanding of Language Arts and literacy education?

7. In what other disciplines can these strategies be incorporated, and what might their use look like across the curriculum?

8. What strategies can you think of, based on the principles involved in these activities, to encourage more multimodal, transmediational thinking and learning across the curriculum?

9. What political problems (e.g., resistance from those who might view these activities as "just play") do you anticipate from using such strategies, and how do both individual teachers and larger groups of teachers defend their instruction in the face of criticism?

10. How might drama and theater be further transmediated through musical reading and expression of the sort explored in the first part of this chapter?

11. How do existing means of evaluating teacher quality fit with Tamiqua's instruction?

12. If existing means of evaluation miss the mark, what kind of teacher evaluation system would faithfully assess the quality and impact of her instruction?

REFERENCES

Au, K., & Valencia, S. (2010). Fulfilling the potential of standards-based education: Promising policy principles. *Language Arts, 87*(5), 373–380.

Bamberger, J. S. (1995). *The mind behind the musical ear: How children develop musical intelligence.* Cambridge, MA: Harvard University Press.

Barton, D., & Hamilton, M. (2000). Literacy practices. In D. Barton, M. Hamilton, & R. Ivanic (Eds.), *Situated literacies: Reading and writing in context* (pp. 7–15). New York, NY: Routledge.

Bolton, G. (1984). *Drama as education: An argument for placing drama at the centre of the curriculum.* London, UK: Longman.

Educational Arts Team. (2008–2011). *Theater strategies: A U.S. Department of Education AEMDD project to improve teaching methods and increase student learning through the infusion of theater arts standards with language arts and literature.* Jersey City, NJ: Author. Retrieved from http://educationalartsteam.com/wp-content/uploads/2013/06/TS_3_YEAR_REPORT_N.pdf

Fueyo, J. (1991). Reading "literate sensibilities": Resisting a verbocentric writing classroom. *Language Arts, 68*(8), 641–648.

Garton, A., & Pratt, C. (1998). *Learning to be literate: The development of spoken and written language* (2nd ed.). Indianapolis, IN: Wiley-Blackwell.

Gordon, E. (1970). *Iowa tests of music literacy.* Chicago, IL: GIA Publications.

Gordon, E. (1988). *Learning sequences in music: Skill, content, and patterns: A music learning theory.* Chicago, IL: GIA Publications.

Green, L. (2001). *How popular musicians learn.* London, UK: Ashgate.

Green, L. (2008). *Music, informal learning and the school: A new classroom pedagogy.* London, UK: Ashgate.

Harste, J., Woodward, V., & Burke, C. (1984). *Language stories and literacy lessons.* Portsmouth, NH: Heinemann.

Heath, S. B. (1986). Sociocultural contexts of language development. In S. B. Heath (Ed.), *Beyond language: Social and cultural factors in schooling language minority students* (pp. 143–186). Sacramento, CA: California State Department of Education, Sacramento, Bilingual Education Office. [ED 304 241]

Jourdain, R. (1997) *Music, the brain, and ecstasy: How music captures our imagination.* New York, NY: William Morrow and Company.

Machover, T. (2002). Instruments, interactivity, and inevitability. *Proceedings of the 2002 Conference on New Instruments for Musical Expression (NIME-02),* Dublin, May 24–26, 2002. Retrieved July 23, 2012, from http://www.suac.net/NIME/NIME02/machover_keynote.pdf

Morrell, E. (2002). Toward a critical pedagogy of popular culture: Literacy development among urban youth. *Journal of Adult and Adolescent Literacy, 46*(1), 72–77.

The New London Group. (1996). A pedagogy of multiliteracies: Designing social futures. *Harvard Educational Review, 66,* 60–92.

Nordoff, P., & Robbins, C. (1977). *Creative music therapy: Individualized treatment for the handicapped child.* New York, NY: John Day.

Siegel, M. (2006). Rereading the signs: Multimodal transformations in the field of literacy education. *Language Arts, 84,* 65–77.

Smagorinsky, P. (2001). If meaning is constructed, what is it made from? Toward a cultural theory of reading. *Review of Educational Research, 71,* 133–169. Retrieved from http://www.petersmagorinsky.net/About/PDF/RER/RER2001.pdf

Strand, K. (2006). Survey of Indiana music teachers on using composition in the classroom. *Journal of Research in Music Education, 54*(2), 154–167.

Strand, K., & Larsen, L. (2011). A Socratic dialogue with Libby Larsen on music, musical experience in American culture, and music education. *Philosophy of Music Education Review, 19*(1), 52–66.

Suhor, C. (1984). Towards a semiotics based curriculum. *Journal of Curriculum Studies, 16*(3), 247–257.

Tabone, C. (2010). *Bringing literature to life: Theater strategies and sample lesson plans for middle school literacy handbook.* Washington, D.C.: United States Department of Education Arts in Education Model Development and Dissemination Project.

Upitis, R. (1992). *Can I play you my song? The compositions and invented notations of children.* Portsmouth, NH: Heinemann.

About the Contributors

Joseph M. Flanagan completed his BA in English from Augustana College, Rock Island Illinois, his MAT in English from the University of Chicago, and a Certificate of Advanced Study in educational administration from the University of Illinois, Champaign–Urbana, where he is also presently pursuing a doctoral degree in Education, Policy, Organization and Leadership. Joseph is an experienced high school English teacher and administrator. He served as chair of the English Department at York Community High School, Elmhurst, Illinois and the Director of Communication Arts at Adlai E. Stevenson High School, Lincolnshire, Illinois, where he presently teaches full time. His articles have appeared in *English Journal* and *Illinois English Bulletin*. He lives in Elmhurst, Illinois with his wife Nancy, his son David, his daughters Mary and Anne, and their mixed breed hound Padfoot.

Chauncey Monte-Sano is associate professor of Educational Studies at the University of Michigan. A former high school history teacher and National Board Certified teacher, she prepares novice teachers for the history classroom and works with veteran history teachers through a variety of professional development programs. Her research examines how history students learn to reason with evidence in writing, and how their teachers learn to teach such historical thinking. Chauncey has won research grants from the Institute of Education Sciences and the Spencer Foundation, as well as awards from the National Council of the Social Studies and Division K of the American Educational Research Association. She has co-authored *Reading Like a Historian: Teaching Literacy in Middle and High School History Classrooms* (2011) with Sam Wineburg and Daisy Martin as well as *Reading, Thinking, and Writing about History: Teaching Argument to Diverse Learners in the Common Core Classroom, Grades 6 –12* with Susan De La Paz and Mark Felton (2014).

Denise Miles is a high school teacher at a public school in Calvert County Maryland. She has been teaching high school Social Studies courses for the last eight years. She also teaches courses in a career pathway program aimed towards high school students who plan to pursue careers in education. Throughout her time in Calvert County, she has developed and implemented various professional develop sessions involving historical literacy. During the 2007–2008 school year, she worked on a disciplinary literacy project at the University of Maryland. During this project, she helped to design primary source based lessons and facilitate professional development for local teachers. Over the years, she has served as a teaching assistant to several Social Studies methods courses at the University of Maryland. Most recently, Denise was involved in a Teaching American History Grant funded project with Prince Georges County teachers and the University of Maryland. Along with a colleague, she has also presented at two Maryland Council for the Social Studies conferences. Her presentations include "teaching history with the senses" and "using primary sources to invigorate the classroom." Denise is also an active member in the National Council for the Social Studies.

Kok-Sing Tang, Ph D., is an Assistant Professor at the National Institute of Education, Singapore in the Natural Sciences and Science Education Department. Prior to joining NIE, he taught Physics and Project Work at Tampines Junior College and worked as an Educational Technology Officer at the Ministry of Education. Kok–Sing has also taught Classroom Management and ICT for Meaningful Learning as a teaching fellow at NIE, and is currently the program coordinator for the Master of Education in Science. His research focuses on a range of topics, from the inward analysis of science classroom discourse to the outward exploration of out-of-school connections. He also studies the micro-genetic development of knowledge and identity construction in science, and studies the design of pedagogy concerning popular media for meaningful science learning and 21st century critical learning. Kok–Sing has received an award for the NTU Overseas Graduate Scholarship in Singapore, as well as the PSC Overseas Merit Scholarship.

Stephen C. Tighe is a physics teacher and science department chair at Lake Orion High School in Lake Orion, Michigan. He received both his Bachelor of Science in Education and Masters of Arts in Interdisciplinary Science from Wayne State University in Detroit, Michigan. Stephen began his teaching career in 1999 as the science teacher in an interdisciplinary "school within a school" program for 10th and 11th grade students. Here he got to work closely with an ELA, Social Studies, and Business teacher integrating curriculum. It was here where he first began observing disciplinary specific literacy practices outside of science. Stephen's passion for science literacy began when he started working with the Oakland Writing Project, a local site of the National Writing Project. Through the Oakland Writing Project he was introduced to co-author Kok–Sing Tang. Kok–Sing completed his doctoral research in Steven's physics classroom. Steven regularly facilitates science and literacy focused professional development for his intermediate school district as well as at regional and state conferences.

Elizabeth Birr Moje is the associate dean for research and community engagement and an Arthur F. Thurnau Professor in the School of Education at the University of Michigan. She also serves as a faculty associate in the university's Institute for Social Research, Latino/a Studies, and in the Joint Program in English and Education. Elizabeth studies the intersection between the disciplinary literacies of school and the literacy practices of youth outside of school. In addition, she studies how youth draw from home, community, ethnic, popular, and school cultures to *make* culture and enact identities. Elizabeth began her career teaching history, biology, and drama at high schools in Colorado and Michigan. Her current research focuses on communities and schools in Detroit, Michigan.

Linda Hutchison, Ph D., is an Associate Professor in the Department of Secondary Education at the University of Wyoming. Her courses focus on quantitative reasoning and mathematics pedagogy, and she has performed extensive research concerning professional development in mathematics for rural teachers in both Wyoming and New Zealand. Linda has acted as a conference chair for the National Council of Teachers of Mathematics Regional conference, and is a member of the American Educational Research Association, as well as the National Council of Teachers for Mathematics. She has served for the Department of Education, and has acted as the Editorial Board reviewer for the International Electronic Journal of Mathematics Education, citing her interest the integration of technology into mathematics teaching. Linda is an established author, having published *Arithmetic Teacher, Mathematics Teaching in the Middle School, Early Childhood Education Journal, Encyclopedia of Mathematics Applications* and *Teacher Education Quarterly.*

Jennifer Edelman is currently an assistant professor of secondary education at the University of West Georgia. She worked with Linda Hutchison while earning her Ph.D. in Curriculum and Instruction: Mathematics Education, centering her dissertation on the use of children's literature in learning to teach mathematics. Jennifer's research interests extend to the use of technology in the classroom and on policies surrounding education reform. While working as a teacher at the elementary school level, she also worked as a lead mentor, math and technology leader, and research dissemination coach. Jennifer has published several projects, centered on topics ranging from empirical support for the use of children's literature in mathematics to exploring the nostalgia in education reform and policy.

Karinna Riddett-Moore, Ph.D., is currently the visual arts instructor for the Atlanta Speech School, the nation's most comprehensive center for language and literacy. There she teaches an integrated arts curriculum, emphasizing visual literacy with the goal of developing an ethic of care through classroom environment and pedagogy. She is motivated by the premise that the arts are necessary in education because they provide students with a means to explore their world and recognize the significance of their own experiences. Her work within the field of arts-based educational research utilizes her identities as artist, researcher, and teacher within the context of living inquiry. Her a/r/tographic study on the nature of caring won three national awards, including the Eliot Eisner Doctoral Research Award in Art Education. Her research interests include arts-based inquiry, aesthetic theory, poststructural theory, narrative and poetic writing, experiential curriculum, and best practices in working with students with language-based processing disorders and students who are deaf or hard of hearing. She lives in Atlanta, Georgia with her husband and two sons and is an avid runner.

Richard Siegesmund is Professor of Art+Design Education at Northern Illinois University and holds a Ph.D. in Art Education from Stanford University. His research interests are in arts-based research and aesthetics as a philosophy of care. With Melisa Cahnmann-Taylor, he co-edited *Arts-Based Research in Education: Foundations for Practice* and his journal articles have appeared in *Phi Delta Kappan, Studies in Art Education*, and the *International Journal of Art & Design Education*. He is also a former President of Integrative Teaching International, an organization that seeks to reimagine the first-year learning outcomes of post-secondary art and design education. He was a Fulbright Scholar and has received fellowship awards from the Getty Education Institute for the Arts, the National Endowment for the Arts, and the University of Georgia's Willson Center. A Distinguished Fellow of the National Art Education Association, he is also is a recipient of the organization's Manuel Barkan Memorial Award for significance of published research. Currently, he also serves as a Research Associate to the Research Institute of the National College of Art and Design, University College Dublin, Ireland.

Katherine D. Strand is an Associate Professor of Music in the Jacobs School of Music at Indiana University where she teaches classes in general music education methods, curriculum, inclusive music practices, and qualitative research methods. She taught K–12 choral and general music in Virginia and the Chicago public schools as well as serving as choral director for the Virginia Governor's School for the Visual and Performing Arts and Humanities for eight years. Katherine has presented workshops on teaching language literacy through musical creativity and composition in the choir classroom at both state and national conferences. Her research interests include creativity, multicultural music pedagogy, and arts integration curricula. In addition to authoring several book chapters, Katherine's research and pedagogical articles have appeared in *Music Educators Journal, Teaching Music, General Music Today*, the *Journal of Research in Music Education, Bulletin of the Council for Research in Music Education, Journal of Music Teacher Education, Philosophy of Music Education Review, Music Education Research*, and the *Indiana Musicator*.

Gus Weltsek is the coordinator of the Indiana University Drama and Theater in Education License Program, as well as the Ivy Tech Community College–Bloomington Theater and Arts Integration Curriculum Development Specialist for the Ivy Tech John Waldron Arts Center. Most recently named to the National Coalition for Core Arts Standards, Gus serves on the Theater Writing Team. His interests focus on making art an integral piece of thinking about and understanding education, from a point of view that stems from pedagogy of social justice and equity. Gus has led pre-service teachers at the IU School of Education to form the Arts in Education Club, has hosted a series of dramatic performance technique workshops, and continuously performs research on the benefits of infusing the arts into school curriculums.

Index

CORWIN

A SAGE Company

The Corwin logo—a raven striding across an open book—represents the union of courage and learning. Corwin is committed to improving education for all learners by publishing books and other professional development resources for those serving the field of PreK–12 education. By providing practical, hands-on materials, Corwin continues to carry out the promise of its motto: **"Helping Educators Do Their Work Better."**

Ingram Content Group UK Ltd.
Milton Keynes UK
UKHW050210110723
424873UK00008B/135

9 781452 229935